STILLNESS

Practicing the Presence of God
in a Restless World

Ruth Conlon

Eternal*life*
Publishers

EternalLife Publishers is a publishing ministry with a passion for spiritual development. We produce individual and group resources to accompany you on your sacred journey. For more information on our training and products, go to www. pursuingholiness.org. EternalLife Publishers is the publishing arm of Pursuing Holiness Ministries.

Email: info@pursuingholiness.org

Published by EternalLife Publishers, a part of Pursuing Holiness Ministries

London, England

www.pursuingholiness.org

Book Layout by EternalLife Publishers

Cover designed by EternalLife Publishers

Stillness / Ruth Conlon. —1st Ed.

ISBN 978-0-9934696-7-1

Table of Contents

Introduction to the Devotional

We live in a world that rarely pauses. A world that measures value by velocity—how fast we produce, how quickly we respond, how constantly we remain connected. In this culture of hyperactivity, stillness can feel foreign, even frightening. Yet, within the noise and rush, the soul begins to whisper a deeper need—something ancient, sacred, and essential. A longing not for more doing, but for deeper being.

This devotional is your invitation to step away from the tyranny of busyness and into the gentle embrace of stillness. It is not about escape, but encounter. Not about isolation, but intimacy. It is an invitation to practice the presence of God—not just occasionally, but daily, rhythmically, and authentically.

Stillness is not a performance or a spiritual technique. It is a posture of the heart. It is where we stop striving and start listening. Where we trade hurry for holiness, and worry for worship. In stillness, we meet the God who does not shout over the noise but whispers in the quiet. The One who is not absent in the silence, but profoundly present.

Each day of this devotional offers you more than words—it offers you space. Space to breathe, reflect, pray, and simply be with God. You will journey through Scripture meditations, thoughtful reflections, soul-stirring questions, and simple practices that lead you gently into sacred pause. Some entries will bring comfort; others may challenge. But all are crafted to draw your soul closer to the One who is already near.

In the quiet, transformation begins. Not in the whirlwind, but in the whisper. Not through control, but through surrender.

So let us begin—not by striving, but by stilling. Let us enter the holy hush. Let us dare to believe that in the stillness, we will find not emptiness, but Emmanuel.

You are not behind. You are not forgotten. You are invited.

Come, beloved.

Be still—and know.

THE CALL TO STILLNESS

1

The Invitation to Stillness

Scripture Meditation

"Be still, and know that I am God." — Psalm 4610 (NIV)

There is an invitation echoing through the ages—one not loud or forceful, but gentle, persistent, and soul-stirring. God calls us into stillness. In a world intoxicated with noise and motion, stillness can feel unnatural. Yet it is in stillness that we become most aware of the eternal. It is the womb where revelation is birthed.

Stillness is not the absence of activity—it is the presence of attentiveness. It is not emptiness—it is sacred space, filled with divine presence. It is the pause where eternity seeps into time and where your soul aligns with the rhythms of heaven.

The Spirit of God is inviting you to step off the treadmill of performance and enter into a slower, more sacred pace. Not just with your feet, but with your heart. Stillness is not just something you do; it is something you become.

Reflection Questions

- When was the last time you truly felt still before God?
- What distractions or internal noise do you need to surrender?

Practice for Today

Find a quiet space. Set a timer for five minutes. Sit in silence. Breathe deeply and slowly. With each breath, invite God to reveal Himself in the stillness. Don't strive to hear—just be.

God's presence is not far off; He is here in the quiet.

Prayer

Lord, I accept Your invitation into stillness. Quiet my anxious thoughts, and tune my ears to the whisper of Your Spirit. Teach me the art of being present with You. Let me know You, not just in the noise of worship or the rush of ministry, but in the still, sacred hush where You dwell. Amen.

2

God's Whisper in the Wind

Scripture Meditation

"After the earthquake a fire, but the Lord was not in the fire; and after the fire a still small voice." — 1 Kings 1912 (NKJV)

In the drama of life, we often look for God in the loud, the big, the extraordinary. We expect Him to thunder through the skies or blaze through the fire. Yet, like Elijah on Mount Horeb, we are brought to the edge of revelation only to discover that God is not in the earthquake or fire—but in the whisper.

God's voice, more often than not, comes in a form that requires our quietness to perceive it. He whispers because He is close. A whisper demands our leaning in, our stillness, our full attention. He invites us to tune out the chaos and train our hearts to listen for the subtle, sacred sound of His presence.

Stillness sharpens our hearing. It makes our soul sensitive to the nuances of divine communication. In the whisper, there is both tenderness and power—an intimate encounter with the God who chooses to be near.

Reflection Questions

- Have you been waiting to hear God in dramatic ways?
- How might you tune your heart to recognize His whisper today?

Practice for Today

Spend ten minutes in silence today. As you sit quietly, picture yourself like Elijah in the cave—waiting, listening. Don't rush. Simply say, 'Speak, Lord, your servant is listening,' and wait. Journal anything that stirs in your heart.

Stillness is not doing nothing—it is doing the holy work of being.

Prayer

Lord, help me to recognise Your whisper in the wind. Teach me to value stillness, to lean in when You speak softly. Make my soul sensitive to Your nearness. May I not miss You by looking only for the spectacular, but find You in the sacred simplicity. Amen.

3

Silence before the Storm

Scripture Meditation

"The Lord will fight for you; you need only to be still." — Exodus 1414 (NIV)

There's a moment before breakthrough that often feels like nothing is happening. A hush, a pause, a breath held in eternity. This is the silence before the storm. Not the chaos of destruction, but the storm of divine deliverance—when God steps in to move on our behalf.

Israel stood between an advancing army and a blocked sea. Their fear rose, their panic stirred. But God's command was simple Be still. In that stillness, God revealed His power. The sea parted not in their striving, but in their surrender.

We often want to act, to fix, to run. But there are battles we are not called to fight—only to witness. Stillness, in these moments, becomes an act of trust. It is the posture that declares, 'God, I believe You are working even when I can't see it.'

Reflection Questions

- Are there areas in your life where God is asking you to be still?
- What fears rise up when you stop trying to control the outcome?

Practice for Today

Bring a current storm or struggle before God. Instead of asking Him to change it immediately, sit in silence and surrender it. Let your stillness be your trust. Repeat, 'The Lord will fight for me; I need only to be still.'

Stillness is not doing nothing—it is doing the holy work of being.

Prayer

Father, help me to rely You in the waiting. When storms approach, remind me that silence is not absence, but anticipation. Help me to stay still, rooted in faith, watching for Your hand to move. You are my defender and deliverer. Amen.

4

The Restless Heart

Scripture Meditation

"You will keep in perfect peace those whose minds are steadfast, because they trust in you." — Isaiah 263 (NIV)

Restlessness is often the background noise of our lives—a low hum of unease that never fully quiets. It shows up in our constant need to check, to scroll, to move, to achieve. And yet underneath all of it is a soul longing for rest in something sure, steady, and sacred.

The restless heart is not a problem to fix—it's a signpost pointing toward what is missing. St. Augustine wrote, 'Our hearts are restless until they rest in You, O Lord.' Only God can satisfy the ache. Only His presence brings the kind of peace that quiets the noise inside.

Stillness exposes the restlessness. It shows us the undercurrent we've learned to ignore. But it also becomes the place of healing. When we choose stillness, we begin to train our hearts to be anchored, not in activity or affirmation, but in the abiding presence of God.

Reflection Questions

- In what areas of your life do you feel most restless right now?
- What would it look like to trust God more deeply in those areas?

Practice for Today

When you feel the urge to reach for your phone or fill a quiet moment with activity, pause. Breathe. Whisper the name of Jesus. Let that moment become an altar where restlessness is surrendered.

You are invited into rest, not because you're finished, but because you are His.

"In the cell of your soul, listen for the still, small voice." – St. Teresa of Avila

Prayer

Lord, my heart is often restless, searching for comfort in all the wrong places. Draw me back to You. Be my still point in the storm, my anchor in every moment. Quiet my soul with Your peace. Amen.

5

Be Still and Know

Scripture Meditation

"Be still, and know that I am God." — Psalm 4610 (NIV)

There is a knowing that only comes through stillness. It's not the knowing of facts or theology alone—it's the knowing born of encounter. When we are still, our hearts become tender soil for divine revelation. We move beyond theory into trust. Beyond anxiety into awareness.

Psalm 46 speaks of chaos—nations in uproar, mountains falling, waters roaring. And yet, right in the middle of that storm, God invites 'Be still.' He doesn't say, 'Be strong.' He says, 'Be still and know.'

To know God is not to grasp Him with intellect, but to experience Him with our entire being. It requires presence. It requires surrender. Stillness becomes the sacred space where knowing unfolds—not in control, but in communion.

Reflection Questions

- What does 'knowing God' mean to you today?
- How can you shift from striving to stillness in your relationship with Him?

Practice for Today

Read Psalm 46 slowly. As you reach verse 10, pause and read it aloud multiple times. Let the words settle into your soul. Write down what God might be revealing to you in that stillness.

God's presence is not far off; He is here in the quiet.

Prayer

God, I want to know You—not just with my mind but with my heart. Teach me to be still. Teach me to trust. In the quiet, show me who You are. Let my stillness become the place where I encounter Your presence. Amen.

6

Elijah in the Cave

Scripture Meditation

> "Then he went into a cave and spent the night. And the word of the Lord came to him 'What are you doing here, Elijah?'" — 1 Kings 199 (NIV)

Elijah, the bold prophet who had called down fire from heaven, now finds himself hiding in a cave. He's exhausted, disillusioned, afraid. Stillness finds him not in strength, but in surrender.

God doesn't rebuke Elijah's weariness. Instead, He meets him in the silence with a question 'What are you doing here?' It's not a question of condemnation, but of invitation. An invitation to reflect, to realign, to reconnect.

We all have caves—places where fear, burnout, or disappointment drive us inward. But God's voice finds us there. And it's often in the stillness of those hidden places that our deepest healing begins. Stillness isn't always chosen. Sometimes it's where God finds us when we've run out of strength.

Reflection Questions

- Are you in a 'cave' season right now—emotionally, spiritually, or physically?
- What might God be asking you in this place of stillness?

Practice for Today

Spend time journaling with this question 'What are you doing here?' Let God use it to reveal what's beneath the surface. Don't rush to fix—just listen and reflect.

You are not behind—God meets you right where you are.

Prayer

Lord, thank You for meeting me in the cave. Thank You for not abandoning me in my exhaustion or fear. Speak to me in this stillness. Ask me what I've been afraid to face, and help me answer honestly in Your presence. Amen.

7

The Still Small Voice

Scripture Meditation

"And after the fire came a gentle whisper." — 1 Kings 1912 (NIV)

The voice of God is not always found in what is loud or dramatic. Elijah discovered this when God bypassed the wind, the earthquake, and the fire—and came instead in a gentle whisper. A still small voice.

That voice requires a different kind of listening. It calls for us to tune our ears and still our hearts. It is not a voice that competes for attention but one that waits for us to slow down.

This whisper reveals the tenderness of God. He could thunder if He wanted, but often chooses to speak in a way that draws us closer. In the stillness, His whisper speaks comfort, guidance, and truth. Are you quiet enough to hear it?

Reflection Questions

- What distractions might be keeping you from hearing God's whisper?
- When have you experienced God's voice in a gentle, subtle way?

Practice for Today

Spend five minutes in quiet prayer. Don't speak. Don't ask. Simply sit in God's presence and say, 'Speak, Lord.' Notice what rises in your heart during this stillness.

You are invited into rest, not because you're finished, but because you are His.

Prayer

Whispering God, quiet my spirit so I can hear You. Remove the noise of fear, doubt, and striving. Help me lean into Your gentleness. May Your still small voice become the loudest truth in my life. Amen.

8

Jesus and Solitude

Scripture Meditation

"But Jesus often withdrew to lonely places and prayed." — Luke 516 (NIV)

Jesus—the Son of God, full of power and purpose—made solitude a regular rhythm in His life. He didn't retreat out of weakness, but out of wisdom. He knew that intimacy with the Father required withdrawal from the crowds.

In the quiet places, Jesus was renewed, refocused, and reconnected. He didn't wait until burnout forced Him into silence. He chose it. Solitude wasn't isolation—it was communion.

In following Jesus, we follow Him not just in ministry, but in rhythm. If He needed the quiet place, so do we. Stillness is not an optional extra for the spiritual life—it is essential. It is there we hear, heal, and align again with God's will.

Reflection Questions

- How often do you intentionally withdraw for time alone with God?
- What might change in your life if solitude became a sacred rhythm, not just a reaction to exhaustion?

Practice for Today

Carve out 15 minutes today to be completely alone with God. No phone. No agenda. Just you and Him. Let it be a time of silent presence. Let Him restore and realign you.

There is no rush. Heaven moves at the pace of peace.

Prayer

Jesus, You showed me the way to live a life of intimacy with the Father. Help me not to avoid solitude but to embrace it. Draw me to quiet places. Let me find my strength not in constant doing, but in communion with You. Amen.

9

The Desert Fathers

Scripture Meditation

"Therefore I am now going to allure her; I will lead her into the wilderness and speak tenderly to her." — Hosea 214 (NIV)

In the early centuries of Christianity, men and women left the chaos of cities to seek God in the desert. They became known as the Desert Fathers and Mothers. Their goal wasn't escape—it was encounter. In solitude, they sought the voice of God.

They discovered what still holds true today in the wilderness, distractions fall away. In the silence, God speaks. The desert became their sanctuary, a place of purification, transformation, and deep listening.

We don't all need to flee to the wilderness. But we can learn from their longing. Stillness often feels like a desert at first—empty, uncomfortable. But if we stay, it becomes holy ground. God still meets His people in the quiet wild.

Reflection Questions

- What can you learn from the way the Desert Fathers and Mothers pursued stillness?
- What might your own 'desert' space look like in your current life?

Practice for Today

Take a walk in silence—no phone, no music. Let it become your wilderness walk. As you move, imagine God drawing near, speaking tenderly. Let the silence guide your soul into stillness.

Your soul is safe in the hands of the One who formed it.

"To one who has faith, no explanation is necessary. To one without faith, no explanation is possible." – St. Thomas Aquinas

Prayer

God of the desert, lead me into the quiet where You speak. Strip away my distractions, and help me embrace the sacred wilderness. May I learn to meet You not just in the crowd, but in the quiet. Amen.

10

Learning to Wait

Scripture Meditation

"I wait for the Lord, my whole being waits, and in his word
I put my hope." — Psalm 1305 (NIV)

Waiting is not a passive posture—it is one of the most spiritually active things we do. In waiting, our trust is tested, our priorities are revealed, and our hearts are refined. Stillness and waiting go hand in hand.

We want answers quickly. We want movement. But God often works in the unseen places of delay. He does His deepest work in us while we're standing still. Waiting is where faith becomes more than words—it becomes surrender.

When we learn to wait with hope, we develop a stillness rooted in assurance, not anxiety. God is never late. His timing trains us to trust Him, not just His answers. And in the quiet of the wait, we come to know Him more deeply.

Reflection Questions

- What are you currently waiting on God for?
- How can you shift from impatience to hope-filled stillness during the wait?

Practice for Today

Write down a situation where you are waiting for God to move. Sit quietly with it before Him. Don't ask Him to act—just acknowledge the wait and offer it as worship. Let the waiting become your prayer.

God's presence is not far off; He is here in the quiet.

Prayer

God of perfect timing, teach me to wait well. Let stillness become my place of strength. I trust You with my unmet prayers, my delays, and my unknowns. As I wait, may I grow in faith, hope, and peace. Amen.

11

Sabbath _ A Rhythm of Stillness

Scripture Meditation

"Then God blessed the seventh day and made it holy, because on it he rested from all the work of creating that he had done." — Genesis 23 (NIV)

Before humanity did anything—before sin entered the story, before toil and pain—God established rest. Sabbath wasn't a reaction to burnout; it was part of the rhythm of creation. A holy pause, woven into the fabric of life.

Stillness has always been God's idea. It reminds us that we are not machines, nor are we gods. We are creatures—created to rest, to receive, to enjoy. In Sabbath, we remember who we are and who we are not.

Sabbath is a sacred protest against productivity as identity. It tells the world, and our own souls, that we are loved not for what we do, but for who we are in God. Stillness becomes sacred when we learn to honour rest as worship.

Reflection Questions

- How do you currently view rest and Sabbath?
- What changes can you make to honour a rhythm of stillness in your weekly life?

Practice for Today

Choose a time in your week to practice Sabbath—no work, no striving, just rest. Reflect on God's goodness. Let that space become holy ground where you are reminded God is in control, and you are held.

There is no rush. Heaven moves at the pace of peace.

Prayer

Lord of rest, teach me to honour Your rhythm of stillness. Help me to step away from the grind and step into grace. In my rest, may I find You waiting—ready to restore, renew, and remind me of who I am in You. Amen.

12

Inner Noise and External Chaos

Scripture Meditation

"In repentance and rest is your salvation, in quietness and trust is your strength, but you would have none of it." — Isaiah 3015 (NIV)

The world outside is loud, but often the greater noise is within. Thoughts that race, fears that echo, voices from the past, pressures from the present. We crave silence, yet we carry chaos in our souls.

Isaiah's words are both a promise and a warning. Strength is found not in more effort, but in quietness and trust. But how often do we resist this invitation? We choose movement over stillness, noise over silence, control over surrender.

To truly dwell in stillness, we must face both the noise around us and the noise within. As we do, God meets us—not with condemnation, but with calm. He teaches us to quiet our souls and rest in His unshakable presence.

Reflection Questions

- What inner noise has been dominating your thoughts lately?
- How can you begin to silence that chaos with trust in God?

Practice for Today

Take 10 minutes of silence today. As thoughts come up, don't fight them. Gently lay each one before God, saying, 'I trust You with this.' Let your inner world become a sanctuary of surrender.

There is no rush. Heaven moves at the pace of peace.

Prayer

God of peace, calm the chaos within me. Teach me to release my anxious thoughts and trust You deeply. Let my soul be stilled by Your presence, even when the world around me is loud. I choose rest. I choose You. Amen.

13

Contemplation and Stillness

Scripture Meditation

"One thing I ask from the Lord, this only do I seek that I may dwell in the house of the Lord all the days of my life, to gaze on the beauty of the Lord and to seek him in his temple." — Psalm 274 (NIV)

Contemplation is more than thinking deeply—it is beholding. It is fixing the eyes of our soul on God, not to analyze Him, but to adore Him. It is the stillness that leads to wonder.

David's longing in Psalm 27 was not for answers, but for presence. To gaze upon God's beauty. Contemplation requires stillness, for beauty is not rushed. It is savoured.

In the busyness of life, we forget to behold. We look, but we do not see. We move, but we do not dwell. Stillness reorients us. It slows us down enough to notice God again—to be captured, captivated, and changed.

Reflection Questions

- When was the last time you simply beheld God's beauty without asking for anything?
- What distractions need to be set aside so you can contemplate deeply today?

Practice for Today

Set a timer for 10 minutes. Read Psalm 274 slowly, out loud. Then sit in silence and picture yourself gazing on the beauty of God. Don't rush. Let awe take over.

Your soul is safe in the hands of the One who formed it.

Prayer

Lord, I want to behold You—not just study or serve You, but gaze upon You in stillness. Restore my wonder. Let my heart be drawn into holy contemplation. May Your beauty silence every other noise. Amen.

14

Living Attentively

Scripture Meditation

> "The Sovereign Lord has given me a well-instructed tongue, to know the word that sustains the weary. He wakens me morning by morning, wakens my ear to listen like one being instructed." — Isaiah 504 (NIV)

Stillness is not just a moment—it is a way of being. Living attentively means being fully present, fully engaged, and fully aware of God's movements throughout the day. It means noticing the gentle nudges, the quiet voice, the divine interruptions.

Isaiah describes a disciple who listens morning by morning. Not rushed, not distracted, but tuned in. Attentiveness begins in stillness, but it carries into action. It changes how we speak, how we walk, and how we respond.

To live attentively is to live awake—to God, to others, and to your own soul. It is the fruit of a life rooted in presence.

Reflection Questions

- Where is God calling you to be more attentive today?
- What might you notice if you slowed down and listened more carefully?

Practice for Today

Take a slow walk or sit outside. Pay attention to your surroundings. Breathe deeply. As you do, ask God, 'What do You want me to notice today?' Write down what He reveals.

God's presence is not far off; He is here in the quiet.

"To one who has faith, no explanation is necessary. To one without faith, no explanation is possible." – St. Thomas Aquinas

Prayer

God, awaken my senses. Help me live with a heart that listens and eyes that see. Let my life be marked by holy attentiveness—to You, to others, and to the beauty hidden in the ordinary. Amen.

15

A Theology of Rest

Scripture Meditation

"Come to me, all you who are weary and burdened, and I
will give you rest. Take my yoke upon you and learn from
me, for I am gentle and humble in heart, and you will find
rest for your souls." — Matthew 1128–29 (NIV)

Rest is not a luxury—it's a divine invitation. Jesus doesn't call the
busy to do more, but to come closer. His rest isn't just physical; it's
soul-deep. It's a rest that comes from being known, loved, and carried.

A theology of rest affirms that God is not impressed by our constant
movement. He designed us to rest as a rhythm of trust. To rest is to
say, 'I believe You are enough. I don't have to strive for what You've
already secured.'

Stillness, then, is an act of faith. It reflects the very nature of God who
rested on the seventh day—not out of fatigue, but delight. And He
invites us into that same rhythm of delight, dependence, and divine
restoration.

Reflection Questions

- How do you define rest in your spiritual life?
- Where might God be inviting you to surrender striving and
  receive His rest?

Practice for Today

Write down three areas where you are striving. Offer them to Jesus. Meditate on His words in Matthew 1128-29. Let His promise of rest settle over your soul like a warm blanket.

Stillness is not doing nothing—it is doing the holy work of being.

Prayer

Jesus, You invite me into Your rest—not because I've earned it, but because You love me. Help me to receive it. Break the patterns of striving in me and restore my soul with the stillness that only You can give. Amen.

16

Finding God in the Pause

Scripture Meditation

"The Lord is good to those whose hope is in him, to the one who seeks him; it is good to wait quietly for the salvation of the Lord." — Lamentations 325–26 (NIV)

Pauses can feel uncomfortable. We are conditioned to fill every gap, every silence, every lull. But in the kingdom of God, pauses are sacred. They create space for awareness, reflection, and intimacy.

Lamentations reminds us that hope and quietness go hand in hand. The pause is not a place of emptiness, but of expectancy. It's where God shows up—not always with answers, but always with presence.

Finding God in the pause means learning to stop resisting it. To welcome the gap between action and outcome, between question and answer. Stillness in the pause becomes the soil for deep trust and divine encounter.

Reflection Questions

• How do you typically respond to moments of pause or delay?
• What would it look like to embrace them as opportunities for deeper connection with God?

Practice for Today

Throughout your day, notice the pauses—between tasks, in conversations, during transitions. Instead of rushing through them, whisper a prayer 'God, I welcome You here.' Let the pauses become holy.

There is no rush. Heaven moves at the pace of peace.

Prayer

Lord, help me to stop filling every silence. Teach me to be present in the pauses, to hear Your whisper there. Let my soul grow still and receptive, that I may encounter You in the quiet spaces of my life. Amen.

17

Letting Go of Hurry

Scripture Meditation

"There is a time for everything, and a season for every activity under the heavens." — Ecclesiastes 31 (NIV)

Hurry is the enemy of spiritual depth. It steals our peace, numbs our sensitivity to God, and crowds out meaningful connection. We rush because we fear falling behind, missing out, or losing control. But in Christ, we are not driven—we are led.

Ecclesiastes reminds us that life has seasons. Each one with its own pace, its own grace. Learning to embrace God's timing helps us release the frantic striving.

Stillness invites us to let go of the hustle. To believe that we're not held together by productivity, but by presence. And when we slow down, we discover a life that is not just fuller—but holier.

Reflection Questions

- What drives your hurry—fear, pressure, or comparison?
- Where might God be inviting you to slow down and live more deeply?

Practice for Today

Choose one task today to do slowly and intentionally—without multitasking or rushing. Let it be an act of worship. Notice how slowing down affects your awareness of God's presence.

You are not behind—God meets you right where you are.

Prayer

God, I confess my addiction to hurry. Teach me to walk at the pace of Your grace. Help me to rest in the rhythm You've set for my life. Let stillness become my way of trusting You. Amen.

18

Trusting in God's Timing

Scripture Meditation

"But they who wait for the Lord shall renew their strength;
they shall mount up with wings like eagles; they shall run
and not be weary; they shall walk and not faint." — Isaiah
4031 (ESV)

Trusting God's timing requires surrender. It means acknowledging
that His plans are better—even when they don't align with our own.
Stillness teaches us to wait well, to listen deeply, and to lean into the
mystery of divine timing.

Isaiah reminds us that waiting isn't weakness—it's strength. It's the
place where God exchanges our exhaustion for His power. We rise
not by rushing, but by resting in His promise.

When we trust His timing, we stop forcing doors open and start
watching for His movement. Stillness shifts our pace to His. And in
His perfect time, He renews, restores, and reveals.

Reflection Questions

- Where are you struggling to trust God's timing in your life?
- How can stillness help you surrender control and embrace His
  pace?

Practice for Today

Reflect on a situation where you feel delayed or discouraged. Offer it to God in prayer. Say, 'I trust Your timing.' Write down one way you will choose patience over striving today.

Stillness is not doing nothing—it is doing the holy work of being.

Prayer

Father, I lay down my timetable and take up Your peace. Teach me to trust You in the waiting. Help me walk in step with Your Spirit, not ahead or behind. I rest in Your perfect timing. Amen.

19

Peace That Surpasses Understanding

Scripture Meditation

"And the peace of God, which transcends all understanding, will guard your hearts and your minds in Christ Jesus." — Philippians 47 (NIV)

God's peace isn't logical. It doesn't always make sense in the face of what we're facing. But that's exactly what makes it holy. It's not the absence of trouble, but the presence of Someone greater than our trouble.

This peace comes not from control or certainty, but from surrender. It arrives when we choose prayer over panic, presence over pressure. And it guards us—not with force, but with quiet assurance.

Stillness is the doorway to this peace. When we pause, breathe, and turn our hearts toward Christ, we receive what only He can give peace that holds us, even when everything else is shaking.

Reflection Questions

- Where do you need God's peace to guard your heart and mind today?
- How can you practice stillness as a way to receive His peace more fully?

Practice for Today

Take five minutes to sit quietly with your hands open. As you breathe in, say, 'Your peace.' As you breathe out, say, 'Surpasses understanding.' Let His peace wash over you in the stillness.

There is no rush. Heaven moves at the pace of peace.

"We need to find God, and he cannot be found in noise and restlessness." – Mother Teresa

Prayer

Prince of Peace, I surrender my anxious thoughts to You. Guard my heart and mind. Still my soul with Your nearness. Let Your peace be the anchor in every storm I face. Amen.

20

Mindfulness in the Spirit

Scripture Meditation

"The mind governed by the Spirit is life and peace." — Romans 86 (NIV)

Mindfulness, when rooted in the Spirit, is not about emptying the mind but filling it with awareness of God's presence. It's a sacred attentiveness that turns ordinary moments into encounters with the divine.

The world teaches us to be mindful for productivity or stress relief— but the Spirit teaches us to be mindful for communion. To live with the Spirit is to live aware, aligned, and awake to God's constant nearness.

Stillness helps us recalibrate our minds. We learn to set them not on the flesh, but on the Spirit—where life and peace abound. When our thoughts dwell in Him, even chaos cannot steal our clarity.

Reflection Questions

- How often are your thoughts governed by the Spirit throughout your day?
- What habits can help you cultivate Spirit-led mindfulness in your life?

Practice for Today

Choose a daily task—washing dishes, brushing your teeth, walking. Do it slowly, with full awareness of God's presence. As you move, whisper, 'Holy Spirit, govern my thoughts.' Let this become a moment of mindfulness in the Spirit.

Stillness is not doing nothing—it is doing the holy work of being.

Prayer

Holy Spirit, fill my mind with peace and life. Teach me to be mindful of You in every breath, every task, every conversation. Let my stillness be soaked in awareness of Your presence. Amen

PRACTICES OF PRESENCE

21

Mary at the Feet of Jesus

Scripture Meditation

"Mary has chosen what is better, and it will not be taken away from her." — Luke 1042 (NIV)

In a culture of performance, the stillness of Mary can seem passive or unproductive. But Jesus saw her posture for what it truly was devotion. While Martha moved and served, Mary sat—listening, learning, loving.

Jesus didn't correct her choice; He affirmed it. 'She has chosen what is better.' Stillness at His feet is not laziness—it is spiritual hunger. It's the quiet pursuit of intimacy.

We all have Martha moments, but we are invited into Mary moments. Not to abandon service, but to anchor it in presence. Stillness positions us to receive what truly cannot be taken away—communion with Christ.

Reflection Questions

- Do you find it hard to sit still with Jesus? Why or why not?
- What would it look like for you to choose 'what is better' today?

Practice for Today

Take 15 minutes today to sit quietly with the story of Mary and Martha (Luke 1038–42). Read it slowly. Imagine yourself in the room. Choose to sit at Jesus' feet and listen.

Stillness is not doing nothing—it is doing the holy work of being.

Prayer

Jesus, I want to choose what is better. Draw me out of my busyness and into Your presence. Help me to sit, to listen, and to love You with stillness. Let nothing steal my attention from You. Amen.

22

Cultivating Quietude

Scripture Meditation

"Make it your ambition to lead a quiet life You should mind your own business and work with your hands, just as we told you." — 1 Thessalonians 411 (NIV)

Quietude is more than silence—it's a spiritual posture. It's an inward calm, a holy steadiness, a refusal to be shaken by the noise of the world. It must be cultivated intentionally, as one plants seeds in a garden.

Paul's words to the Thessalonians remind us that ambition isn't always about rising louder or higher. Sometimes, the most countercultural thing we can do is to lead a quiet life—a life that listens, loves, and labours in peace.

Stillness teaches us that quietude isn't weakness. It's strength under the Spirit's control. It is where we hear God best, speak less, and live wisely.

Reflection Questions

- What habits or thoughts disrupt your inner quietude?
- How might you embrace a quieter rhythm of life, inwardly and outwardly?

Practice for Today

Choose one moment of your day to do in complete silence—no background noise, no distractions. Let it be an act of worship. Ask God to deepen your inner quietude as you go about your task.

You are seen, known, and loved—even in your silence.

Prayer

Lord, teach me the strength of quietude. Still my heart from constant noise. Help me cultivate a spirit of peace that reflects Your character. May my life be rooted in Your rest, not in the rush of the world. Amen.

23

Stillness in Suffering

Scripture Meditation

"The Lord will fight for you; you need only to be still." —
Exodus 1414 (NIV)

Suffering shakes us. It brings questions, pain, and sometimes silence. In those moments, stillness can feel like abandonment. But in the quiet ache, God draws near.

When Israel stood at the Red Sea, surrounded by danger, God didn't tell them to act—He told them to be still. It was in that stillness that His power was revealed. The sea parted. The way was made.

Stillness in suffering doesn't mean denying your pain. It means anchoring your soul in God's presence while the storm rages. It means trusting that He sees, He knows, and He will move. Even when words fail, stillness can speak your faith.

Reflection Questions

• Where are you experiencing suffering or silence from God?
• What would it look like to choose stillness instead of striving in this season?

Practice for Today

Take a few minutes to sit with your pain in God's presence. You don't need to explain it. Just bring it. Say 'Lord, I am here. I trust You to be here too.' Let your stillness be your surrender.

You don't have to earn God's nearness—just receive it.

Prayer

God of comfort, meet me in the stillness of my suffering. I don't always understand, but I choose to trust. Be my refuge, my healer, and my hope. Hold me in the silence, and lead me in Your peace. Amen.

24

Dwelling in the Secret Place

Scripture Meditation

"Whoever dwells in the shelter of the Most High will rest in the shadow of the Almighty." — Psalm 911 (NIV)

The secret place is not a physical location—it's a posture of the heart. It's the inner sanctuary where your soul meets God. It's stillness that becomes sanctuary.

To dwell is to stay, to remain, to be rooted. The secret place is not a quick visit—it's a life lived near to God. It's where fears are silenced, where strength is renewed, and where identity is affirmed.

In stillness, we find the shadow of the Almighty—a covering that is both powerful and tender. He draws us into His presence not just for protection, but for communion. The secret place is open to all who choose to dwell.

Reflection Questions

*   What does the 'secret place' mean to you personally?
*   How can you create space each day to dwell rather than rush past God's presence?

Practice for Today

Create a quiet space—physically or internally—where you can meet with God. Sit in stillness and whisper Psalm 911. Let yourself rest in the shadow of the Almighty and simply be with Him.

"God is found in the silent places." – Thomas Merton

Stillness is not weakness; it is strength in surrender.

Prayer

Most High God, draw me into Your secret place. Let me not just visit Your presence but dwell in it. Teach me to remain in Your shadow, to find rest and refuge in You alone. I choose to stay near. Amen.

25

Awareness of God's Nearness

Scripture Meditation

"The Lord is near to all who call on him, to all who call on him in truth." — Psalm 14518 (NIV)

Sometimes we imagine God is distant—up in the heavens, far from our everyday lives. But Scripture reminds us again and again He is near. Near to the brokenhearted. Near to the humble. Near to those who call.

Stillness sharpens our awareness. It doesn't make God come closer— it simply awakens us to the reality that He's already here. In the quiet, we begin to feel His nearness, sense His whisper, and notice His movement.

You don't have to earn God's presence. You only have to become aware. The invitation to stillness is an invitation to open your eyes to the nearness of a God who has never left.

Reflection Questions

- When have you felt most aware of God's presence in your life?
- What distracts you from sensing His nearness in everyday moments?

Practice for Today

Take a few minutes to sit quietly and repeat the phrase 'God, You are near.' Breathe deeply and allow this truth to settle in your spirit. Notice how it shifts your awareness throughout the day.

You don't have to earn God's nearness—just receive it.

Prayer

Lord, thank You that You are always near. Help me to be still long enough to see, hear, and feel You. Let my awareness of Your nearness become the peace I walk in today. Amen.

26

The Fruit of Silence

Scripture Meditation

"Even fools are thought wise if they keep silent, and discerning if they hold their tongues." — Proverbs 1728 (NIV)

Silence may seem empty, but spiritually, it is full of potential. In silence, the heart listens. In silence, wisdom grows. In silence, God speaks in ways that words can't always capture.

Proverbs reminds us that even the appearance of silence carries weight. How much more when it is a silence filled with the presence of God? Stillness is the soil where spiritual fruit begins to form—love, patience, self-control, peace.

When we make room for silence, we don't just hear better—we become better. The fruit of silence is not found in the sound of our voices, but in the transformation of our hearts.

Reflection Questions

- What type of spiritual fruit has grown in you during seasons of silence?
- How might you invite more fruitful silence into your current routines?

Practice for Today

Spend ten minutes today in complete silence. No prayers, no words—just you and God. Afterwards, journal any insight, peace, or fruit that emerged.

You are seen, known, and loved—even in your silence.

Prayer

Lord, thank You for the gift of silence. Let it not be empty or fearful, but full of Your Spirit. Grow in me the fruit that comes from listening more and speaking less. Amen.

27

Sacred Spaces

Scripture Meditation

"This is what the Sovereign Lord says In repentance and rest is your salvation, in quietness and trust is your strength." — Isaiah 3015 (NIV)

Sacred spaces are not defined by architecture—they are formed by presence. Wherever we meet with God, wherever we pause to listen, to rest, to worship—that place becomes holy.

Stillness creates sacred space. It sets the atmosphere for divine encounter. Whether it's a corner of your room, a spot in nature, or the hush before dawn, these places become altars where heaven meets earth.

The more we intentionally create sacred spaces in our lives, the more we cultivate a heart that's constantly aware of God's nearness. We don't need a temple—we are the temple. Stillness reminds us of that truth and invites us to live it daily.

Reflection Questions

- Where in your life or home could you create a sacred space for meeting with God?
- How have certain physical places helped shape your spiritual journey?

Practice for Today

Designate a small area as your sacred space—light a candle, clear the clutter, or simply sit quietly. Invite God's presence and dedicate that space as holy ground.

Peace is not the absence of problems; it's the presence of God.

Prayer

Holy God, thank You that You meet me wherever I make room for You. Teach me to create sacred spaces—not just around me, but within me. Let every pause, every quiet moment, become a sanctuary. Amen.

28

Discerning God's Voice

Scripture Meditation

"My sheep listen to my voice; I know them, and they follow me." — John 1027 (NIV)

God is always speaking—but are we still enough to hear Him? His voice is not confined to burning bushes or booming thunder. Often, it comes as a whisper, a nudge, a scripture recalled in the quiet.

Jesus says His sheep know His voice. That kind of knowing takes time, attention, and stillness. We learn to discern His voice by spending time in His presence, soaking in His Word, and tuning our ears to the tone of love.

Stillness sharpens our spiritual hearing. It makes room for the voice of God to cut through the noise and lead us in truth.

Reflection Questions

- What does God's voice sound like in your life—how do you recognise it?
- What noise in your environment or heart needs to be quieted to hear Him more clearly?

Practice for Today

Spend time in silence, asking God to speak. Read John 1027 slowly. Then write down what you sense He might be saying. Trust His voice. Lean into what brings peace, conviction, and clarity.

You are not behind—God meets you right where you are.

Prayer

Good Shepherd, I want to hear You clearly. Quiet every competing voice and tune my heart to Yours. Let Your Word dwell richly in me and guide me in every step. Amen.

29

The Solitude of Christ

Scripture Meditation

"Very early in the morning, while it was still dark, Jesus got up, left the house and went off to a solitary place, where he prayed." — Mark 135 (NIV)

Jesus sought solitude—not just once, but regularly. In the midst of miracles, crowds, and constant need, He withdrew. He made space to commune with the Father, to be refreshed, to realign with His mission.

Solitude was not isolation—it was communion. It wasn't escapism— it was engagement with the deepest source of strength.

Stillness calls us to follow Christ not just in public faith, but in private retreat. If Jesus needed solitude to thrive spiritually, so do we. Let His rhythm guide our own. In the quiet, we return to the centre of all things—God Himself.

Reflection Questions

- How often do you intentionally withdraw for time alone with God?
- What hinders you from practising solitude as Jesus did?

Practice for Today

Choose a time today to retreat to a quiet place, even for ten minutes. Leave your phone behind. Bring your Bible or a journal. Let your solitude become sacred space with God.

Your soul is safe in the hands of the One who formed it.

"He who does not find God in the silence is unlikely to find Him elsewhere." – Meister Eckhart

Prayer

Jesus, You modelled the beauty and necessity of solitude. Help me follow Your example. Draw me into quiet places, where I can meet You and be renewed. Let my soul be shaped in the silence. Amen.

30

Learning to Linger

Scripture Meditation

"Better is one day in your courts than a thousand elsewhere;
I would rather be a doorkeeper in the house of my God than
dwell in the tents of the wicked." — Psalm 8410 (NIV)

In a world of speed and multitasking, lingering feels inefficient.
But spiritually, lingering is where transformation begins. To
linger in God's presence is to prioritise presence over productivity,
communion over completion.

Psalm 84 is the heart cry of one who longs not just to visit God's
presence, but to remain there—to dwell, to wait, to linger. It is in
this posture that our love deepens, our strength is renewed, and our
vision becomes clear.

Stillness creates space to linger. Not to rush in and out, but to
wait until our hearts settle, until we hear His whisper, until we are
changed.

Reflection Questions

- What keeps you from lingering in God's presence?
- How might lingering more intentionally change the depth of
  your relationship with Him?

Practice for Today

Spend extra time today in God's presence. When you feel ready to leave, stay five minutes longer. Ask God to meet you in that lingering—and watch what unfolds.

Your soul is safe in the hands of the One who formed it.

Prayer

Lord, teach me to linger. Slow me down. Increase my hunger for more of You. Let my time in Your presence be unhurried and deep. Meet me in the stillness and transform me by Your love. Amen.

31

Stillness as Resistance

Scripture Meditation

"Do not conform to the pattern of this world, but be transformed by the renewing of your mind. Then you will be able to test and approve what God's will is—his good, pleasing and perfect will." — Romans 122 (NIV)

In a world that glorifies hustle, stillness becomes a radical act. It is a protest against the tyranny of busyness and a declaration that our value is not in what we produce, but in who we are before God.

To be still is to resist the current of culture. It is to choose depth over distraction, worship over worry, and communion over chaos.

Paul's words in Romans 12 call us not to conform, but to be transformed. That transformation begins in the quiet places. Stillness becomes a battleground and a sanctuary—where the noise of the world is silenced and the whisper of God becomes our guide.

Reflection Questions

- In what ways has the world's pace shaped your identity or self-worth?
- How can stillness become your daily act of resistance and renewal?

Practice for Today

Turn off your devices for one hour today. Let that silence be a statement 'I belong to God, not to this world's demands.' Use that time to sit with Him, journal, or rest in His presence.

You don't have to earn God's nearness—just receive it.

Prayer

Lord, I resist the pull of hurry and performance. I choose stillness. Renew my mind, reshape my values, and restore my soul. Let my stillness honour You and reflect Your kingdom. Amen.

32

Holy Indifference

Scripture Meditation

"I have learned the secret of being content in any and every situation whether well fed or hungry whether living in plenty or in want. I can do all this through him who gives me strength." — Philippians 4:12–13 (NIV)

Holy indifference is not apathy—it is detachment rooted in trust. It means being so anchored in God that we are not swayed by outcomes, status, or external success. It is the spiritual posture that says, 'Your will be done,' and truly means it.

Paul had learned to be content whether in abundance or lack. His stillness was internal. It did not depend on conditions around him, but on the presence within him.

Stillness helps us cultivate this holy indifference. It frees us from the grip of needing to control, impress, or possess. It teaches us to hold everything lightly and to cling only to God.

Reflection Questions

- Where in your life are you clinging too tightly to outcomes or expectations
- How might God be inviting you into a holy indifference grounded in trust

Practice for Today

Identify one area where you're emotionally attached to a specific result. In prayer, release it to God. Say aloud, 'I trust You more than I trust the outcome.' Let stillness reset your heart.

Peace is not the absence of problems; it's the presence of God.

Prayer

Father, I surrender my desire for control. Teach me the strength of holy indifference. May my joy not rise and fall with circumstances, but stay anchored in You. Help me to live freely, fully, and faithfully. Amen.

33

Practicing Peace

Scripture Meditation

"Let the peace of Christ rule in your hearts since as members of one body you were called to peace. And be thankful." — Colossians 3:15 (NIV)

Peace is not something we stumble into by accident. It is cultivated. Practicing peace means actively choosing it—aligning our thoughts, our breath, and our focus with the Prince of Peace.

Paul says to let the peace of Christ rule in our hearts. That means we have a choice in what governs us. We can let worry rule—or peace. Fear—or trust.

Stillness trains us to let peace take the lead. It teaches our hearts how to exhale fear and inhale truth. And as we do, peace moves from a fleeting feeling to a steady practice rooted in Christ.

Reflection Questions

- What tends to rule in your heart when life gets busy or stressful
- How can you actively practice peace throughout your day

Practice for Today

Pause during the day to check in with your heart. Ask yourself, 'Is peace ruling here' If not, pause and pray, inviting Christ to take His rightful place as your peace.

Peace is not the absence of problems; it's the presence of God.

Prayer

Jesus, let Your peace be the ruler of my heart. When stress rises or fear creeps in, remind me to pause. Let stillness become my way of returning to You. I choose Your peace. Amen.

34

The Spiritual Discipline of Listening

Scripture Meditation

"Speak Lord for your servant is listening." — 1 Samuel 3:10 (NIV)

Listening is more than hearing. It is a sacred posture. One of attentiveness, humility, and surrender. Samuel's simple response became a model for all of us who long to hear God's voice—'Speak Lord, for your servant is listening.'

Listening requires stillness. It requires us to quiet our inner dialogue, set aside our agendas, and create space for God to speak. It is both an art and a discipline, shaped over time through practice and presence.

Stillness trains our ears. It teaches us to recognise the Shepherd's voice, even when it whispers through silence.

Reflection Questions

• How often do you stop to listen rather than speak when you pray
• What helps or hinders your ability to hear God's voice clearly

Practice for Today

Begin your prayer time today with silence. Say only, 'Speak Lord, I am listening.' Then wait. Don't rush to fill the space. Let your listening be an act of faith.

Your soul is safe in the hands of the One who formed it.

"In the cell of your soul, listen for the still, small voice." – St. Teresa of Avila

Prayer

Lord, tune my ears to hear You. Teach me the discipline of listening— not just for guidance, but for relationship. May Your voice be clearer than all others in my life. Amen.

35

Abiding in His Presence

Scripture Meditation

"Remain in me as I also remain in you. No branch can bear fruit by itself it must remain in the vine. Neither can you bear fruit unless you remain in me." — John 15:4 (NIV)

Abiding is not a one-time visit—it is a continuous dwelling. Jesus invites us into a relationship that is rooted, enduring, and life-giving. To abide is to stay connected to His presence, not just in prayer, but in every part of life.

Stillness teaches us to remain. When we abide, we do not strive to be fruitful—we simply stay close to the Vine. And from that connection, life flows.

Abiding means we carry His presence into our routines, our relationships, and our thoughts. We live from the inside out—anchored in intimacy with Christ.

Reflection Questions

- What does abiding in Christ look like in your daily routine
- Where do you feel disconnected and how might stillness restore that connection

Practice for Today

Choose one activity today—work, walking, eating—and do it with
an awareness that you are abiding in Christ. Repeat in your heart, 'I
remain in You.' Let that awareness deepen your connection.

Stillness is not doing nothing—it is doing the holy work of being.

Prayer

Jesus, help me remain. Let my soul cling to You in the quiet and the
busy, in joy and in strain. Teach me to abide—not with effort, but
with love. Let fruitfulness be the overflow of our intimacy. Amen.

36

Saint Teresa of Avila and Interior Castle

Scripture Meditation

"The kingdom of God is within you." — Luke 17:21 (KJV)

Saint Teresa of Avila described the soul as an interior castle made of crystal. At its centre dwells the King. Stillness, for her, was the way to journey deeper—through the rooms of distraction, pain, and purification—into the heart of God.

Her writings remind us that the inner life is not flat. It is layered, expansive, and holy. To enter into stillness is to begin the pilgrimage inward. Not to escape the world, but to find God dwelling in the centre of our being.

Stillness is the sacred hallway through which we travel from surface to centre. It is where intimacy is nurtured, transformation happens, and divine union is made possible.

Reflection Questions

- How does the image of an interior castle shape your view of the spiritual life
- What 'rooms' do you sense God inviting you into right now

Practice for Today

Take five minutes of silence today. Imagine yourself entering the interior castle of your soul. Walk toward the centre where God is waiting. Let His presence draw you deeper inward.

You don't have to earn God's nearness—just receive it.

Prayer

Lord, lead me through the inner chambers of my soul. Strip away distraction and fear. Help me to dwell in the centre with You. Let my stillness become sacred ground where I know and am known. Amen.

37

The Monastic Call to Silence

Scripture Meditation

"Set a guard over my mouth Lord keep watch over the door of my lips." — Psalm 141:3 (NIV)

For centuries, monastic communities have embraced silence as a spiritual discipline. Not as punishment, but as communion. They understood what we often forget—God speaks most clearly when we stop speaking.

Silence in the monastic life is sacred. It is woven into daily rhythm, creating space for deep listening, prayer, and contemplation. It teaches self-control, fosters humility, and opens the heart to God.

Stillness draws us into that same monastic spirit. We may not live in a monastery, but we can carry the discipline of silence into our lives. A few quiet moments, intentionally kept, can echo the depth of centuries of devotion.

Reflection Questions

- What might silence teach you that words cannot
- How could you incorporate small moments of monastic silence into your daily routine

Practice for Today

Set aside a brief period—perhaps between tasks or meals—to be completely silent. Let that moment become an act of worship and listening. Resist the urge to fill the space. Let silence speak.

Stillness is not doing nothing—it is doing the holy work of being.

Prayer

Lord of silence and speech, teach me the wisdom of restraint. Help me create sacred space with my silence. Let my quiet moments draw me deeper into You. Amen.

38

The Watch of the Night

Scripture Meditation

"On my bed I remember you I think of you through the watches of the night. Because you are my help I sing in the shadow of your wings." — Psalm 63:6–7 (NIV)

There is a sacred hush that settles over the world at night. While others sleep, the soul often stirs—yearning, watching, waiting. The night watch has long been a time of holy attentiveness for saints and seekers.

David speaks of remembering God in the watches of the night. These moments are not just for sleep, but for secret encounters. In the silence of night, our distractions fade and the voice of God grows clearer.

Stillness in the night is a powerful offering. It is worship wrapped in darkness, longing laced with love. When you rise to pray or pause in those hours, know this—you are not alone. Heaven watches with you.

Reflection Questions

- Have you ever experienced the presence of God in the night
- How might you turn restless nights into moments of sacred stillness

Practice for Today

Set your alarm to wake for a brief moment during the night. Use that time to whisper a prayer, read a psalm, or sit quietly with God. Let your night become an offering of stillness and trust.

God's presence is not far off; He is here in the quiet.

Prayer

God of the night watch, meet me in the quiet hours. Let my rest be wrapped in Your nearness. When I awaken, help me turn my thoughts to You. May even my nights be filled with worship. Amen.

39

Trusting God in the Unknown

Scripture Meditation

> "Trust in the Lord with all your heart and lean not on your own understanding in all your ways submit to him and he will make your paths straight." — Proverbs 3:5–6 (NIV)

The unknown often brings fear. We crave control, certainty, and clarity. But God calls us to something deeper—trust.

To trust in the unknown is to release the illusion that we must have it all figured out. It is to rest in the truth that God already knows, sees, and leads. Stillness teaches us that trust doesn't grow through answers—it grows through surrender.

When we let go of leaning on our own understanding, we discover the peace of being guided. The quiet path of faith unfolds not with a spotlight, but with the steady light of His presence, one step at a time.

Reflection Questions

- Where in your life are you facing uncertainty or the unknown
- What would it look like to practice stillness and trust in that place?

Practice for Today

Write down a fear or unknown you're currently facing. Offer it to God in prayer. Then sit in silence, repeating the words, 'I trust You with the unknown.' Let peace rise in the stillness.

There is no rush. Heaven moves at the pace of peace.

"In the cell of your soul, listen for the still, small voice." – St. Teresa of Avila

Prayer

Faithful God, You are the same in the mystery as You are in the clear. Help me trust You even when I cannot see. Let stillness be my sanctuary of surrender. Guide me with Your steady hand. Amen.

40

Fasting and Stillness

Scripture Meditation

"Is not this the kind of fasting I have chosen to loose the chains of injustice and untie the cords of the yoke to set the oppressed free and break every yoke" — Isaiah 58:6 (NIV)

Fasting is not just about abstaining from food—it is about making space. It is an invitation to silence, stillness, and greater dependence on God. Fasting quiets the appetites that compete for our attention and makes room for a deeper hunger to arise.

Isaiah reminds us that true fasting leads to freedom. Not just personal, but communal. Fasting and stillness together break the yokes that burden us—the yoke of hurry, distraction, and self-reliance.

In the quiet of fasting, God speaks. In the stillness of hunger, we hear the cry of justice and the whisper of His Spirit. Let your fasting be more than a practice—let it be a doorway into sacred stillness and holy clarity.

Reflection Questions

- What do you need to fast from to create space for God's voice
- How has fasting shaped your ability to listen and surrender in stillness

Practice for Today

Choose one thing to fast from today—whether food, media, or distraction. In the space it creates, sit in stillness with God. Ask Him to meet you in the quiet and show you what freedom looks like.

There is no rush. Heaven moves at the pace of peace.

Prayer

God who frees and fills, I come to You in hunger. I lay down distractions and desires to draw nearer to You. In the stillness of my fasting, speak to me. Shape me. Set me free. Amen.

STILLNESS IN THE STORM

41

The Purifying Fire of Quiet

Scripture Meditation

"He will sit as a refiner and purifier of silver he will purify the Levites and refine them like gold and silver." — Malachi 3:3 (NIV)

Quiet is not always comfortable. It can stir things we've buried, expose fears we've hidden, and bring to the surface the parts of us that still need healing. But this is where the refining begins.

Malachi paints a picture of God as a Refiner—deliberate, gentle, and unrelenting. In the furnace of stillness, He burns away what is not eternal. Not to harm us, but to purify us.

Stillness invites us to sit in the fire—not with dread, but with hope. The heat may rise, but so does the clarity. What remains is gold. What remains is holy. Let the quiet refine you.

Reflection Questions

• What surfaces in you when you sit in silence with God
• How might stillness be refining your heart in this season

Practice for Today

Sit in stillness for ten minutes. As thoughts or emotions rise, invite God to purify your heart. Don't judge what appears—simply offer it to Him and trust in His refining love.

Peace is not the absence of problems; it's the presence of God.

Prayer

Refining God, meet me in the quiet. Burn away what is not of You. Purify my motives, cleanse my desires, and draw me closer to Your likeness. Let the fire of stillness make me holy. Amen.

42

God in the Ordinary

Scripture Meditation

"Surely the Lord is in this place and I was not aware of it."
— Genesis 28:16 (NIV)

We often look for God in the extraordinary—miracles, mountaintops, divine encounters. But God is also in the ordinary. In laundry folded, meals prepared, and walks taken. In conversations and quiet commutes.

Jacob awoke to the realisation that the place he had considered common was in fact sacred. God had been there all along. Stillness sharpens our awareness so we can say the same—'Surely the Lord is in this place.'

Practising stillness helps us live as though every moment matters. Every breath, every glance, every task becomes an opportunity for communion. We begin to find heaven in the ordinary, because God has always been near.

Reflection Questions

- Where in your daily life do you most often overlook the presence of God
- How can stillness help you discover the sacred in the seemingly mundane

Practice for Today

Choose one ordinary task today—washing dishes, answering emails, walking outside—and invite God into it. Say aloud or quietly, 'Surely the Lord is in this place.' Let that truth transform the moment.

You don't have to earn God's nearness—just receive it.

Prayer

God of every moment, open my eyes to see You in the ordinary. Help me not to rush past what is sacred. May stillness awaken my heart to Your nearness in all things. Amen.

43

The Sacredness of Breath

Scripture Meditation

"Then the Lord God formed a man from the dust of the ground and breathed into his nostrils the breath of life and the man became a living being." — Genesis 2:7 (NIV)

Every breath you take is a gift. A reminder that life itself began with the breath of God. Inhaling and exhaling is not just biology—it is holy rhythm. It is the echo of divine life within you.

In stillness, we become aware of this sacred gift. We slow down enough to notice the breath, to appreciate it, and to let it return us to the presence of God. Breath becomes prayer. Breath becomes worship.

When life feels chaotic or disoriented, returning to the breath is a return to God's design. Breathe deeply. God is as close as your next inhale.

Reflection Questions

- How often do you think of your breath as a spiritual practice
- What would it mean for you to honour the breath as a reminder of God's presence

Practice for Today

Set a timer for five minutes. Focus solely on your breathing. As you inhale, say silently 'You give me life.' As you exhale, say 'I rest in You.' Let this become a sacred practice of stillness and gratitude.

You are invited into rest, not because you're finished, but because you are His.

Prayer

Breath of God, thank You for sustaining me with every inhale. Help me slow down and recognise You in each breath. Let my life become worship with every rise and fall of my lungs. Amen.

44

Learning to Be Present

Scripture Meditation

"This is the day the Lord has made let us rejoice and be glad in it." — Psalm 118:24 (NIV)

Presence is a gift, but it is often stolen by distraction. We live fragmented lives—thinking of tomorrow, regretting yesterday, worrying over what's next. But God invites us into today.

Psalm 118 reminds us that this day—not yesterday, not tomorrow— is the day the Lord has made. Stillness roots us in the now. It invites us to fully inhabit this moment, where God is already present and active.

To be present is to honour the sacredness of time. It is to trust that God is working right here, right now. Stillness is how we show up— with our minds, our hearts, and our spirits—in the holy ground of the present.

Reflection Questions

- What distractions most often pull you out of the present moment?
- How does being present help you encounter God more deeply

Practice for Today

Throughout your day, pause and say aloud, 'This is the day the Lord has made.' Let it ground you in the moment. Notice what you see, hear, and feel—embrace this present as a sacred gift.

You are seen, known, and loved—even in your silence.

"Withdraw into yourself and wait patiently." – The Desert Fathers

Prayer

Lord, thank You for this moment. Help me not to miss it. Teach me to live fully present—to You, to others, and to my own soul. Let stillness draw me back to the now, where You are always near. Amen.

45

A Still Heart in a Noisy World

Scripture Meditation

"You will keep in perfect peace those whose minds are steadfast because they trust in you." — Isaiah 26:3 (NIV)

Noise isn't just around us—it lives within us. The hum of anxiety, the chatter of comparison, the echo of expectations. To have a still heart in a noisy world is a miracle of grace and discipline.

Isaiah promises perfect peace to those who are steadfast—those who trust, rest, and remain in God. This peace does not depend on the quietness of our surroundings, but on the rootedness of our soul.

Stillness silences what is loud and amplifies what is eternal. When our hearts are anchored in God, we can carry peace through chaos, clarity through confusion, and calm through every storm.

Reflection Questions

- What inner noise is currently disrupting your peace
- How can you cultivate a still heart even when your environment is loud

Practice for Today

When you feel overwhelmed by noise—external or internal—pause. Take three deep breaths. Repeat Isaiah 26:3 slowly. Let your trust restore your stillness.

You are not behind—God meets you right where you are.

Prayer

God of perfect peace, quiet my restless heart. In the noise of the world and the noise within, be my stillness. Teach me to trust You more deeply, and let that trust become my peace. Amen.

46

The Anchor of Prayer

Scripture Meditation

"Devote yourselves to prayer being watchful and thankful."
— Colossians 4:2 (NIV)

Prayer is not only how we speak to God—it is how we stay connected, grounded, and anchored. In the shifting tides of life, prayer holds us steady.

Paul calls us to be devoted to prayer—not casually engaged, but committed. Prayer becomes the anchor that keeps our hearts near God when storms rise, when distractions come, or when we feel distant.

Stillness enhances our prayer life. It slows us down so we can listen, sense, and respond. It transforms prayer from a rushed monologue into a sacred conversation, rooted in presence and sustained by love.

Reflection Questions

• How has prayer served as an anchor in your life
• What practices help you stay devoted to prayer through different seasons

Practice for Today

Before your day begins or as it ends, spend ten minutes in silent prayer. Don't rush to speak. Just be with God, watchful and thankful, anchored in His presence.

God's presence is not far off; He is here in the quiet.

Your soul is safe in the hands of the One who formed it.

Prayer

Lord, anchor my life in prayer. Let it be my first instinct and my lasting habit. Help me remain steady through every storm, devoted to You in all things. Amen.

47

Patience as Stillness

Scripture Meditation

"Be completely humble and gentle be patient bearing with one another in love." — Ephesians 4:2 (NIV)

Patience is not passive—it is power under restraint. It is the quiet strength to wait, to endure, to trust without rushing. Stillness is often the womb of patience, where character is formed and trust matures.

Paul urges us to be patient not as an afterthought, but as a vital expression of love. When we practice stillness, we learn to wait well. We stop striving to make things happen and begin trusting that God is already at work.

In a world that rewards speed and efficiency, patience is a holy resistance. It's how we live slow enough to love deeply, listen fully, and reflect Christ clearly.

Reflection Questions

- Where in your life do you feel most impatient right now
- How might stillness help you cultivate deeper patience in this season

Practice for Today

Identify a moment when you would normally rush—waiting in line, responding to a message, or finishing a task. Pause instead. Use that moment to breathe and invite God to develop patience in you.

Stillness is not weakness; it is strength in surrender.

Prayer

God of great patience, thank You for bearing with me in love. Teach me to wait with grace, to slow down in trust, and to live gently. Let stillness grow patience in me like fruit ripened in the sun. Amen.

48

Psalm 131 A Weaned Soul

Scripture Meditation

"But I have calmed and quieted myself I am like a weaned child with its mother like a weaned child I am content." — Psalm 131:2 (NIV)

Psalm 131 is one of the shortest psalms, yet it holds a profound picture of spiritual maturity—a soul that is weaned, content, and still. The psalmist speaks not of ambition or striving, but of a quiet trust that resembles a child resting safely in a mother's arms.

A weaned soul no longer demands. It doesn't cling for what it wants. It rests in what is. This is the fruit of stillness—a heart that no longer needs constant reassurance, because it is anchored in God's love.

To be still like a weaned child is to find peace in God's presence, not His provision. It is to embrace the quiet joy of simply being with Him.

Reflection Questions

*   What would it look like for your soul to be truly weaned and content
*   Are there areas where you still cling instead of rest

Practice for Today

Read Psalm 131 aloud slowly. Then sit in silence with God, asking for the grace to be weaned of restlessness, neediness, or control. Let your stillness reflect a quiet trust.

You are seen, known, and loved—even in your silence.

Prayer

Father, calm and quiet my soul. Teach me to rest like a child in Your care. Free me from striving, and lead me into contentment. Let stillness shape in me a heart that is weaned and whole. Amen.

49

Peace in the Midst of Warfare

Scripture Meditation

"The Lord will fight for you you need only to be still." — Exodus 14:14 (NIV)

Stillness does not mean the absence of battle. It means the presence of peace even while the war rages around you. When Israel stood trapped between Pharaoh's army and the Red Sea, God's command wasn't to fight—it was to be still.

Stillness in warfare is not passivity. It is trust. It is choosing not to panic, not to strive, but to believe that God is your defender.

There are moments when your stillness is your weapon. When your calmness is your declaration of faith. Let peace rise, even in the pressure. Your stillness says to the enemy—I know who fights for me.

"Silence is God's first language." – St. John of the Cross

Reflection Questions

- What battles are you facing that tempt you to strive instead of trust
- How does stillness speak as an act of faith in your life right now

Practice for Today

When anxiety rises or conflict flares today, pause. Take three deep breaths. Repeat Exodus 14:14 out loud or in your heart. Let stillness become your strategy and peace your shield.

There is no rush. Heaven moves at the pace of peace.

Prayer

Mighty God, I surrender the battle to You. Teach me to trust You in the middle of the storm. Let my stillness testify of Your strength. Fight for me as I rest in You. Amen.

50

Selah_ The Pause of Worship

Scripture Meditation

"Be still before the Lord and wait patiently for him do not fret when people succeed in their ways when they carry out their wicked schemes." — Psalm 37:7 (NIV)

Throughout the Psalms, the word 'Selah' appears like a holy interruption—a sacred pause. Though its exact meaning is debated, many believe it signals a moment to pause, reflect, and worship.

Stillness and worship are not opposites. In fact, they deepen one another. Worship becomes richer when we stop to remember who God is. Reflection becomes sacred when it leads to adoration.

Selah teaches us that we don't need to rush through praise. We can linger in the moment, soak in the truth, and let it change us. In stillness, our worship finds depth.

Reflection Questions

- How often do you pause during worship to reflect on the truth you're declaring
- What would it look like for you to incorporate moments of Selah into your spiritual rhythm

Practice for Today

Choose one worship song to listen to slowly. After each verse or chorus, pause. Let the words settle in your spirit. Worship not just with song, but with silence.

Stillness is not doing nothing—it is doing the holy work of being.

Prayer

Lord of wonder, teach me to pause in Your presence. Let my worship not be hurried or shallow, but deep and thoughtful. May every Selah lead me into greater awe of You. Amen.

51

Stillness and Discernment

Scripture Meditation

"Whether you turn to the right or to the left your ears will
hear a voice behind you saying This is the way walk in it."
— Isaiah 30:21 (NIV)

Discernment is the art of knowing God's way. It doesn't always come
in flashes of clarity—it often emerges in the quiet. When the heart is
still, the Spirit can lead.

Isaiah 30 speaks of a voice that whispers direction. But to hear that
voice, we must silence the others. Stillness creates space to listen,
reflect, and respond with wisdom rather than reaction.

God's guidance is not always dramatic. It's gentle, faithful, and
consistent. When we live with stillness, discernment becomes less
about guessing and more about abiding. The quiet soul hears clearly.

Reflection Questions

- Where do you need God's direction right now
- How can you make space for stillness as you seek discernment

Practice for Today

Take a question you're facing and bring it to God in silence. Sit quietly for ten minutes, listening. Then write down any impressions, Scriptures, or peace you receive.

Peace is not the absence of problems; it's the presence of God.

Prayer

Guide me Lord. Quiet every competing voice. Help me to hear the whisper of Your Spirit. As I become still, let discernment arise not from fear, but from faith. Amen.

52

Benedictine Practices

Scripture Meditation

"Whatever you have learned or received or heard from me or seen in me put it into practice. And the God of peace will be with you." — Philippians 4:9 (NIV)

The Rule of Saint Benedict offers a rhythm of life built on prayer, work, and sacred rest. His practices remind us that stillness isn't just a feeling—it's a way of life.

Benedict taught stability, humility, and silence. He believed that ordinary tasks could become sacred, and that balance was key to spiritual growth. Stillness in his rule wasn't withdrawal—it was devotion.

We don't need to become monks to live monastically. We can borrow their wisdom to craft daily rhythms that make room for God. Stillness can be woven into our schedule, shaping our soul through repetition and reverence.

Reflection Questions

- What practices in your day could become sacred through intention
- How might you adopt a rhythm that creates space for stillness

Practice for Today

Create a small rule of life for today. Include moments for prayer, silence, work, and rest. Let this rhythm be an act of devotion—a modern echo of Benedictine wisdom.

You are invited into rest, not because you're finished, but because you are His.

Prayer

Lord of rhythm and rest, help me build a life that honours You in all things. Teach me to live with intention and peace. Let stillness mark my days and shape my soul. Amen.

53

Creating Space for God

Scripture Meditation

"Here I am I stand at the door and knock. If anyone hears my voice and opens the door I will come in and eat with that person and they with me." — Revelation 3:20 (NIV)

God desires to dwell with us—but He does not force His way in. He knocks, waits, and invites. Creating space for God is an act of love, a preparation of the soul for divine encounter.

Stillness helps us prepare that space. It clears the clutter, silences the noise, and readies our hearts. When we open the door, we are not just making room—we are making welcome.

Whether it's five minutes in the morning or a sacred rhythm of Sabbath rest, space for God transforms every other part of life. He fills what we offer. He meets us where we wait.

Reflection Questions

- What parts of your life feel too full for God right now
- How can you intentionally make space to welcome His presence

Practice for Today

Clear a physical space—your desk, your room, a corner in your home. Let it be symbolic of your heart. Sit there in stillness, and say, 'Come in, Lord. This space is Yours.'

Stillness is not weakness; it is strength in surrender.

Prayer

Jesus, I open the door. Come and dwell with me. Teach me to create space in my life and in my heart for You. May stillness become a welcome mat for Your presence. Amen.

54

The Ministry of Absence

Scripture Meditation

"But Jesus often withdrew to lonely places and prayed." —
Luke 5:16 (NIV)

"Let nothing disturb you, let nothing frighten you, all things are passing." – St. Teresa of Avila

Absence is not always abandonment. In the spiritual life, absence can be a ministry—a space where we withdraw in order to return refreshed, filled, and realigned.

Jesus modelled this rhythm beautifully. He stepped away from the noise, the crowds, and the demands to be alone with the Father. His absence from people was not neglect—it was preparation.

Stillness sometimes means stepping back. It means choosing solitude not as escape, but as engagement with the One who sends us out again with purpose. The ministry of absence is sacred. It is the space where our souls breathe.

Reflection Questions

- When was the last time you truly withdrew to be with God
- How might stepping back create more space for renewal and clarity in your life

Practice for Today

Choose a time to be absent today—from screens, noise, or interaction. Go to a quiet place, even if for just 15 minutes. Let that absence become a presence before God.

God's presence is not far off; He is here in the quiet.

Prayer

God who meets me in the quiet, teach me the gift of stepping away. Let my absence from the world become deeper connection with You. May I return not empty, but full. Amen.

55

Learning to Withdraw

Scripture Meditation

"Come with me by yourselves to a quiet place and get some rest." — Mark 6:31 (NIV)

Withdrawal is not weakness. It is wisdom. In Mark 6, after ministry and miracles, Jesus invites His disciples to withdraw—not for more action, but for rest.

We often push past our limits, afraid that stepping away might be seen as failure. But stillness teaches us otherwise. It reminds us that our worth is not in doing, but in being.

Withdrawing creates space to reset, to realign, and to renew. It's not abandonment of responsibility—it's the sacred rhythm that allows us to return whole and wholehearted. Let stillness lead you to healthy withdrawal.

Reflection Questions

* Where are you currently being called to withdraw and rest
* What fears do you have about stepping back, and how might God be meeting you in that space

Practice for Today

Take a short walk or sit in a quiet spot today with no agenda. Let your heart exhale. Hear Jesus' invitation, 'Come away with Me.' Receive it with gratitude and peace.

You are invited into rest, not because you're finished, but because you are His.

Prayer

Jesus, thank You for calling me to rest. Give me the courage to withdraw when I need to. Meet me in the quiet place and restore what is weary. May I return with joy, peace, and clarity. Amen.

56

A Silent Cry

Scripture Meditation

"In the same way the Spirit helps us in our weakness. We do not know what we ought to pray for but the Spirit himself intercedes for us through wordless groans." — Romans 8:26 (NIV)

There are moments when words fail. When the ache is too deep, the confusion too loud, and the heart too tender to speak. In those moments, silence is not absence—it is a cry.

Paul writes of the Spirit interceding through groans too deep for words. God hears even the prayers we cannot form. Stillness becomes the language of the soul when our lips fall silent.

Your silence before God is not empty. It is full of longing, trust, and surrender. When you cry without sound, heaven listens. Stillness is not the end of prayer—it is its deepest form.

Reflection Questions

- Have you ever experienced prayer through silence or tears more than words
- What might God be hearing from you in your quiet moments today

Practice for Today

Find a quiet place and sit in silence before God. Do not try to speak or strive. Let your stillness be your offering. Let the Spirit pray through your wordless longing.

You don't have to earn God's nearness—just receive it.

Prayer

Spirit of God, thank You for understanding my silent cries. Meet me in the quiet. Pray through me when I cannot find the words. Let stillness be enough. Amen.

57

Spiritual Retreats

Scripture Meditation

"Very early in the morning while it was still dark Jesus got up left the house and went off to a solitary place where he prayed." — Mark 1:35 (NIV)

Retreats are sacred pauses—intentional withdrawals from the noise of life to encounter the voice of God. Jesus modelled this rhythm, rising early to be alone with the Father. His ministry flowed from intimacy, not busyness.

A spiritual retreat doesn't have to be grand or far away. It is simply a space set apart, where we turn down the volume of the world and tune in to the Spirit. Stillness deepens on retreat. It creates room for rest, renewal, and revelation.

The heart that retreats returns stronger. Take time to step away not as escape, but as encounter. Let stillness wrap you in the presence of God.

Reflection Questions

- When was the last time you retreated for spiritual renewal
- What barriers keep you from creating intentional space to be alone with God

Practice for Today

Block out a few hours—or even just 30 minutes—for solitude this week. Leave your phone behind. Bring your Bible or journal. Let the time be for stillness, not productivity.

God's presence is not far off; He is here in the quiet.

Prayer

Jesus, thank You for inviting me to come away with You. Help me to honour retreat as holy ground. Meet me in stillness, speak into the silence, and restore my soul. Amen.

58

The Discipline of Doing Nothing

Scripture Meditation

"The Lord is good to those who wait for him to the soul who seeks him. It is good that one should wait quietly for the salvation of the Lord." — Lamentations 3:25–26 (ESV)

Doing nothing is not laziness when it is done with intention. In a world addicted to productivity, the choice to be still is radical. It is a discipline that declares—God is enough, even when I am not busy.

The prophet in Lamentations affirms the goodness of waiting quietly. This is the sacred space where striving ceases and seeking begins. Stillness, in its purest form, is not about doing—it is about being.

Let yourself practice this holy discipline. Sit. Wait. Be. Trust that God is at work even when you are not. In stillness, the soul learns to breathe again.

Reflection Questions

- How do you feel when you are doing nothing
- What might God be inviting you to receive in those still and quiet moments

Practice for Today

Set a timer for ten minutes and do absolutely nothing. No phone, no reading, no praying. Just sit and be. Observe what rises in your heart and offer it quietly to God.

Peace is not the absence of problems; it's the presence of God.

Prayer

God of rest, teach me the courage to do nothing. Free me from the tyranny of productivity. Let me find You in the quiet, where nothing is demanded and everything is grace. Amen.

59

Simplicity and Stillness

Scripture Meditation

"Better a little with the fear of the Lord than great wealth with turmoil." — Proverbs 15:16 (NIV)

Simplicity and stillness are close companions. One clears the path, the other walks it. Simplicity quiets the clutter of our lives—possessions, obligations, distractions—so that stillness can thrive.

Proverbs reminds us that peace and reverence are better than abundance with anxiety. The pursuit of more often drowns the voice of God, while simplicity makes room for sacred connection.

Choose less. Choose quiet. Choose room for God. Let simplicity become the soil where stillness can take root and flourish.

Reflection Questions

- What areas of your life feel cluttered or overwhelming
- How might simplifying those areas create space for stillness

Practice for Today

Choose one area—your schedule, a room, a to-do list—and simplify it today. Let go of what is not necessary. Use the space you create to sit with God in stillness.

Peace is not the absence of problems; it's the presence of God.

"We need to find God, and he cannot be found in noise and restlessness." – Mother Teresa

Prayer

God of peace, help me to love simplicity. Free me from the lie that more is always better. Make room in my life for stillness, and in that quiet space, meet me. Amen.

60

Resting in God's Love

Scripture Meditation

"The Lord your God is with you the Mighty Warrior who saves. He will take great delight in you in his love he will no longer rebuke you but will rejoice over you with singing."
— Zephaniah 3:17 (NIV)

There is a kind of rest that cannot be found in a bed or a holiday. It is the rest of being loved. Fully. Deeply. Unconditionally. When you are held in the embrace of God's love, striving ceases and stillness settles in.

Zephaniah gives us a beautiful picture—God not only saves but delights. He rejoices over you. He sings. This is the heart in which you can rest.

Stillness helps us absorb this love. It is not earned by our devotion, it is received in surrender. Let today be a time of simply resting in the joy of being loved by God.

Reflection Questions

- Do you find it easy or difficult to simply rest in God's love without doing anything to earn it
- How might deeper stillness help you experience the delight of God more fully

Practice for Today

Sit in a quiet space today and imagine God rejoicing over you with singing. Let that image settle into your spirit. Say aloud, 'I am loved. I am delighted in.' And rest.

Peace is not the absence of problems; it's the presence of God.

Prayer

Loving God, help me to rest in Your delight. Quiet the voice of earning and let me hear Your song of joy over me. In stillness, may I receive the fullness of Your love. Amen.

RUTH CONLON

SACRED LISTENING
AND DISCERNMENT

61

Reclaiming the Morning

Scripture Meditation

"Let the morning bring me word of your unfailing love for I have put my trust in you. Show me the way I should go for to you I entrust my life." — Psalm 143:8 (NIV)

Mornings set the tone for the day. The way we begin often determines how we carry ourselves through the hours ahead. Stillness in the morning is not just peaceful—it is powerful.

Psalm 143 paints the morning as a moment of divine invitation. It is when our ears are most open, our hearts most tender. Yet so often, we rush. We scroll. We strive.

To reclaim the morning is to give God the first word. It is to sit in silence before Him, receive His love, and be guided by His voice. Let stillness lead your sunrise.

Reflection Questions

- How do you typically begin your mornings and what impact does it have on your day
- What would it look like to reclaim your mornings for stillness and connection with God

Practice for Today

Tomorrow morning, set your alarm 15 minutes earlier. Before checking your phone or jumping into tasks, sit quietly. Read Psalm 143:8. Breathe deeply. Ask God to lead your day from a place of stillness.

God's presence is not far off; He is here in the quiet.

Prayer

Lord of the morning, meet me in the stillness of a new day. Let Your love be the first word I hear. Guide my steps and fill my heart before anything else enters. I entrust this day to You. Amen.

62

Stillness and the Prophetic

Scripture Meditation

"I will stand at my watch and station myself on the ramparts; I will look to see what he will say to me." — Habakkuk 2:1 (NIV)

The prophetic begins in presence. Before words are spoken or visions are seen, there is waiting. Habakkuk stood at his watch—silent, alert, expectant. It was in that posture that the word of the Lord came.

Stillness is the prophetic soil. It tunes our spirits to heaven's frequency and quiets the noise of our opinions. In the hush, we discern what God is truly saying—not just for ourselves, but for others.

To move prophetically is not always to speak loudly. Sometimes it is to listen deeply. Let stillness prepare your heart to hear clearly and speak truthfully.

Reflection Questions

- How has God spoken to you in moments of stillness
- What would it look like to posture yourself in expectation, like Habakkuk, today

Practice for Today

Take time to sit quietly, journal open, heart ready. Say, 'Speak, Lord, Your servant is listening.' Record any impressions, Scriptures, or leadings that arise in the stillness.

You are not behind—God meets you right where you are.

Prayer

God who speaks, I choose stillness to hear You more clearly. Quiet every other voice and align my heart with Yours. Make me a faithful listener and a humble messenger. Amen.

63

God's Timing and Our Hurry

Scripture Meditation

"There is a time for everything and a season for every activity under the heavens." — Ecclesiastes 3:1 (NIV)

We are people of hurry, but God is a God of timing. We rush toward outcomes, grasping at quick answers and instant growth. But heaven's clock is not driven by our deadlines.

Ecclesiastes reminds us that there is a time for everything. Stillness invites us to surrender our pace and embrace divine timing. It teaches us to trust the slow unfolding of God's plan.

When we resist hurry, we begin to move in sync with the Spirit. His pace is patient, purposeful, and perfect. Stillness isn't delay—it's alignment.

Reflection Questions

- Where in your life are you rushing ahead of God's timing
- How can you choose stillness and surrender instead of striving

Practice for Today

Pause during a moment of stress or hurry today. Breathe slowly. Repeat Ecclesiastes 3:1 in your heart. Ask God to help you trust His timing over your urgency.

There is no rush. Heaven moves at the pace of peace.

"He who does not find God in the silence is unlikely to find Him elsewhere." – Meister Eckhart

Prayer

God of seasons and timing, I surrender my hurry to You. Slow me down until my heart matches the rhythm of Yours. Let stillness help me to rely Your perfect pace. Amen.

64

Interior Stillness

Scripture Meditation

"Let the peace of Christ rule in your hearts since as members of one body you were called to peace. And be thankful." — Colossians 3:15 (NIV)

Stillness is more than external quiet. It is an interior state—a calm within the soul that holds steady even when life swirls around you. It is not simply silence, but peace reigning in the heart.

Paul writes that we are called to peace, and not just any peace, but the peace of Christ. This peace does not shift with circumstance; it rules from within. It is an anchor in chaos and a sanctuary in storm.

Interior stillness is cultivated through surrender, gratitude, and presence. As we yield our worries, give thanks, and dwell with God, our inner world begins to mirror His calm.

Reflection Questions

- How often do you experience a deep inner calm regardless of your external circumstances
- What practices help you nurture interior stillness and peace

Practice for Today

Throughout your day, pause and check in with your inner state. Breathe deeply and ask, 'Is peace ruling in my heart right now?' Invite Jesus into any unrest and receive His stillness.

You are invited into rest, not because you're finished, but because you are His.

Prayer

Prince of Peace, let Your calm take root deep within me. Even when life is noisy, let my soul be still. Teach me to carry interior stillness that reflects Your abiding presence. Amen.

65

Letting Go of Control

Scripture Meditation

"Trust in the Lord with all your heart and lean not on your own understanding in all your ways submit to him and he will make your paths straight." — Proverbs 3:5–6 (NIV)

Control is often the enemy of peace. The need to manage every outcome, fix every problem, and predict every step creates anxiety, not stillness. But letting go is where freedom begins.

Proverbs reminds us that trust, not understanding, is the foundation of a directed life. God doesn't ask for our mastery—He asks for our surrender. Stillness is the posture of open hands and a quiet heart.

Letting go is not giving up. It is giving over. It is saying, 'God, I trust You more than I trust myself.' In the release, we find rest.

Reflection Questions

- Where in your life are you trying to maintain control instead of surrendering
- How would letting go bring stillness to your heart

Practice for Today

Write down something you are struggling to control. As an act of surrender, rip up the paper or lay it before God in prayer. Say aloud, 'I let go, and I trust You.'

Peace is not the absence of problems; it's the presence of God.

Prayer

God who sees and knows, I release my grip. I surrender what I cannot fix or understand. Help me to trust You with every path and step. Let stillness come as I let go. Amen.

66

Hospitality to the Presence

Scripture Meditation

"Here I am I stand at the door and knock. If anyone hears my voice and opens the door I will come in and eat with that person and they with me." — Revelation 3:20 (NIV)

Hospitality is more than opening our homes—it's opening our hearts. God desires to dwell with us, but He waits for an invitation. Stillness creates the space to welcome Him in.

Revelation 3 shows Jesus knocking—not forcing His way, but gently seeking access. When we quiet our lives, we begin to hear that knock. We become more attentive to His nearness.

Hospitality to the presence means preparing a sacred space within. It means slowing down long enough to say, 'Come in, Lord.' And when we welcome Him, He brings peace, joy, and fullness with Him.

Reflection Questions

- How are you creating space in your life for God's presence to dwell
- What distractions or clutter might be crowding out His voice

Practice for Today

Light a candle or create a small space of quiet. As you sit, say aloud or in your heart, 'Jesus, You are welcome here.' Let your stillness be an act of holy hospitality.

You are not behind—God meets you right where you are.

Prayer

Jesus, I open the door. I welcome You into the stillness of my soul. Dwell with me, speak to me, and let my heart be a sanctuary for Your presence. Amen.

67

Ancient Practices for Modern Disciples

Scripture Meditation

"Stand at the crossroads and look; ask for the ancient paths ask where the good way is and walk in it and you will find rest for your souls." — Jeremiah 6:16 (NIV)

In an age of innovation and distraction, the ancient paths still lead us to life. Practices like silence, solitude, fixed-hour prayer, and sabbath may feel outdated, but they carry timeless power.

Jeremiah invites us to seek the old ways—not to return to legalism, but to rhythms that have anchored disciples for centuries. Stillness is one of those paths. It slows the soul and tunes it to the voice of the Spirit.

Modern disciples need ancient wisdom. We don't need more noise— we need more presence. Let stillness connect you to the practices that have always drawn hearts to God.

Reflection Questions

- Are there ancient Christian practices you've felt drawn to explore
- How could incorporating one of them draw you into deeper stillness with God

Practice for Today

Choose one ancient practice—like a breath prayer, silence, or praying the Psalms—and try it today. Let it be a doorway into presence, not performance.

You don't have to earn God's nearness—just receive it.

Prayer

God of ages past and present, thank You for the wisdom of the saints. Teach me to walk the ancient paths and find rest for my soul. Let stillness become my way of following You. Amen.

68

Grace in the Waiting Room

Scripture Meditation

"Yet the Lord longs to be gracious to you therefore he will rise up to show you compassion. For the Lord is a God of justice. Blessed are all who wait for him!" — Isaiah 30:18 (NIV)

Waiting rooms are rarely comfortable. They test our patience and remind us that we are not in control. But in God's kingdom, waiting is not wasted—it's a place of grace.

Isaiah reminds us that the Lord longs to be gracious and shows compassion to those who wait. Stillness in the waiting room isn't just about passing time—it's about posturing our hearts in trust.

When we embrace the delay instead of fighting it, we make space to receive. God often works beneath the surface in seasons of waiting. Let stillness be the doorway to deeper grace.

Reflection Questions

- Where in your life are you currently waiting
- How can you see this waiting not as punishment, but as preparation filled with grace

Practice for Today

Spend time reflecting on a waiting season in your life. Write a prayer of surrender and thanksgiving for what God may be doing beneath the surface.

You don't have to earn God's nearness—just receive it.

"He who does not find God in the silence is unlikely to find Him elsewhere." – Meister Eckhart

Prayer

Lord of grace and timing, meet me in the waiting. Help me not to rush ahead or grow bitter in delay. Let stillness open me to the quiet work You are doing in my soul. Amen.

69

The Hidden Life

Scripture Meditation

"For you died and your life is now hidden with Christ in God." — Colossians 3:3 (NIV)

The world celebrates visibility—being known, seen, and applauded. But the kingdom treasures hiddenness. A life anchored in Christ often grows beneath the surface, far from the spotlight.

Paul writes that our life is hidden with Christ in God. This hiddenness is not about obscurity or insignificance—it is about security. In the hidden place, we are protected, refined, and rooted.

Stillness leads us into this secret life. It teaches us to value depth over display, presence over performance. Embrace the hiddenness where God shapes you for things yet unseen.

Reflection Questions

- Do you find yourself longing to be seen or celebrated more than to be hidden in Christ
- How can you embrace the season or calling of hiddenness with peace and trust

Practice for Today

Spend time in stillness without documenting, posting, or sharing it. Let it be a moment just between you and God. Celebrate the unseen space where intimacy grows.

Stillness is not doing nothing—it is doing the holy work of being.

Prayer

God who sees in secret, teach me to love the hidden place. Help me to find joy in being known by You alone. Let stillness draw me deeper into the life that is hidden in Christ. Amen.

70

Stillness as Preparation

Scripture Meditation

"But those who hope in the Lord will renew their strength. They will soar on wings like eagles they will run and not grow weary they will walk and not be faint." — Isaiah 40:31 (NIV)

Before the soaring, there is the stillness. Isaiah 40 reminds us that strength is renewed not in the rush, but in the wait. Stillness is often God's way of preparing us for what's next.

Seasons of silence and solitude are not wasted time. They are divine groundwork. Like a seed buried in the dark soil, something deep is forming even when nothing seems to be happening.

Let stillness shape you for the next step. Trust that what feels like delay may be divine design. In quiet surrender, God prepares you to rise with strength and vision.

Reflection Questions

- Are you in a season that feels still or slow
- What might God be preparing in you beneath the surface

Practice for Today

Write a letter to God thanking Him for this season of preparation, even if you do not yet see the outcome. Offer your stillness as worship and trust.

Stillness is not weakness; it is strength in surrender.

Prayer

God of preparation, thank You for meeting me in the quiet. Shape me in stillness. Form me in faith. And when the time is right, let me soar with You. Amen.

71

Cultivating Peaceful Thoughts

Scripture Meditation

"Finally brothers and sisters whatever is true whatever is noble whatever is right whatever is pure whatever is lovely whatever is admirable if anything is excellent or praiseworthy think about such things." — Philippians 4:8 (NIV)

Our thought life shapes our soul life. Stillness is not only about stopping movement—it is about anchoring the mind. A heart at peace often begins with peaceful thoughts.

Paul calls us to dwell on what is true, noble, and pure. This is not denial of hardship but a discipline of direction. Where the mind dwells, the spirit follows.

Stillness gives space for reflection, not rumination. It invites the Spirit to renew our thinking and anchor us in heavenly perspective. Let your thoughts be a garden where peace grows.

Reflection Questions

- What thoughts tend to dominate your mind during quiet moments
- How can you intentionally choose thoughts that cultivate peace and truth

Practice for Today

Choose one phrase from Philippians 4:8—like 'whatever is lovely'—
and repeat it during your still moments today. Let that truth become
a resting place for your thoughts.

Stillness is not doing nothing—it is doing the holy work of being.

Prayer

God of truth and peace, train my mind to think on what is good and
lovely. When stillness comes, let my thoughts bring life and not fear.
Shape my inner world to reflect Your beauty. Amen.

72

From Anxious to Anchored

Scripture Meditation

"Cast all your anxiety on him because he cares for you." —
1 Peter 5:7 (NIV)

Anxiety often pulls us in a thousand directions. It scatters the soul
and steals our peace. But stillness invites us to cast our cares—not
carry them.

Peter's invitation is both simple and profound: give God what weighs
you down. Not because He is distant, but because He cares. Stillness
becomes a sacred space where burdens are transferred and hearts are
steadied.

Moving from anxious to anchored doesn't always happen instantly.
It's a journey of surrender, breath by breath. Let stillness hold you
long enough to remember—you are not alone.

Reflection Questions

- What anxieties are you currently holding onto
- What would it look like to cast them fully on God today

Practice for Today

Sit quietly with your hands open. Visualise your anxiety and mentally place it in God's hands. Say, 'I give this to You, Lord.' Repeat this practice whenever anxious thoughts arise.

You are not behind—God meets you right where you are.

Prayer

Caring God, I release my worries to You. Anchor me in Your love and peace. Let my anxious heart be calmed in Your presence. Thank You that I am never alone. Amen.

73

Trusting Without Striving

Scripture Meditation

"In repentance and rest is your salvation in quietness and trust is your strength but you would have none of it." — Isaiah 30:15 (NIV)

The world tells us to hustle, but heaven invites us to trust. Isaiah's words cut deep—salvation, strength, and peace are found in quiet trust, not relentless striving.

But how often do we resist this gift? We push, plan, and panic instead of rest. Stillness is the pathway back to trust. It quiets our fears and loosens our grip.

To trust without striving is to believe that God is at work even when we are still. It is the holy surrender that says, 'I believe You are enough.'

Reflection Questions

- Where in your life are you striving instead of trusting
- What would it look like to rest in God's strength instead of your own

Practice for Today

Set aside time to sit quietly with no agenda. As thoughts or worries arise, breathe deeply and whisper, 'I trust You, Lord.' Let this be your response to striving.

Stillness is not doing nothing—it is doing the holy work of being.

"The quieter you become, the more you can hear." – Ram Dass

Prayer

Faithful God, help me to rely without striving. Let my strength be found in stillness. I release my need to perform and prove. You are enough. I rest in You. Amen.

74

Releasing Expectations

Scripture Meditation

"Now to him who is able to do immeasurably more than all we ask or imagine according to his power that is at work within us." — Ephesians 3:20 (NIV)

Expectations can become burdens. When our plans don't unfold the way we imagined, disappointment creeps in. But God often moves beyond our expectations—if we're willing to let them go.

Ephesians 3 reminds us that God does immeasurably more—not always what we pictured, but far beyond in depth, wisdom, and love. Stillness is the space where we release control over how things must look.

When we let go of our expectations, we open our hands to receive what God actually desires to give. And His gifts are always better, deeper, and more eternal than we imagined.

Reflection Questions

- What expectations are you holding tightly that may be limiting your trust in God
- How can releasing those expectations open you up to God's greater work

Practice for Today

Write down one expectation you've been holding onto—about your future, a relationship, or a situation. Offer it to God in prayer and ask Him to replace it with His promise.

Stillness is not doing nothing—it is doing the holy work of being.

Prayer

God who exceeds my imagination, I release my expectations to You. Forgive me for holding tightly to my plans. Shape my heart to trust Your ways, and help me receive the more You have in store. Amen.

75

Stillness in Community

Scripture Meditation

"How good and pleasant it is when God's people live together in unity!" — Psalm 133:1 (NIV)

Stillness isn't only found in solitude—it can also be cultivated in sacred community. When people come together not to perform but to be present, stillness flows between them.

Psalm 133 reminds us of the beauty and blessing of unity. In spiritual community, we learn to listen more than we speak, to hold space for one another, and to encounter God together in silence.

The quiet presence of a friend can become holy ground. Stillness in community teaches us that we don't always need answers—sometimes we just need to be with God and one another, together.

Reflection Questions

- Have you experienced the power of stillness shared with others
- How can your community become a place where peace and presence are nurtured

Practice for Today

Reach out to a trusted friend or small group. Suggest setting aside ten minutes to sit in silence together—no agenda, just presence. See what God does in the quiet between you.

Your soul is safe in the hands of the One who formed it.

Prayer

God of unity and peace, thank You for the gift of others. Teach me to be present in community, not just with words, but with stillness. Let our gatherings reflect Your peace and presence. Amen.

76

Practicing the Presence of God

Scripture Meditation

"Remain in me as I also remain in you. No branch can bear fruit by itself it must remain in the vine. Neither can you bear fruit unless you remain in me." — John 15:4 (NIV)

Brother Lawrence called it 'practicing the presence'—a holy awareness that God is near in every moment. It's not confined to prayer closets or worship services. It's a lifestyle of stillness within.

In John 15, Jesus speaks of remaining—abiding. This is not occasional visiting, but daily dwelling. Stillness becomes the space where we remember that we are always with Him and He with us.

Whether washing dishes, walking the dog, or sitting in silence, practicing His presence changes everything. It's not about trying harder, but tuning in. God is already here.

Reflection Questions

- When are you most aware of God's nearness in your day
- What simple activities could become sacred if you practiced His presence there

Practice for Today

Choose one everyday task—cooking, cleaning, walking—and do it slowly with an awareness of God's presence. Say in your heart, 'You are here, Lord.'

Stillness is not weakness; it is strength in surrender.

Prayer

God who dwells with me always, help me live aware of Your presence. Teach me to abide in You not just in quiet time but in every moment. Let stillness live in my spirit, wherever I go. Amen.

77

Reclaiming Sabbath Joy

Scripture Meditation

"If you call the Sabbath a delight and the Lord's holy day honorable and if you honor it by not going your own way and not doing as you please or speaking idle words then you will find your joy in the Lord." — Isaiah 58:13–14 (NIV)

Sabbath was never meant to be a burden. It is a gift—a sacred rhythm woven into creation for our joy and restoration. Stillness finds its weekly expression in this holy pause.

Isaiah invites us to delight in the Sabbath, to treat it not as legalism but as invitation. In the quiet of Sabbath rest, we remember that God is God and we are not. We cease from striving and make space for joy.

Reclaiming Sabbath joy means resisting hurry, choosing presence, and finding delight in God again. Stillness makes the day holy. Joy makes it whole.

Reflection Questions

- What does Sabbath currently look like in your life
- How might reclaiming its joy restore your soul and still your spirit

Practice for Today

Set aside a few hours this week as a Sabbath window. Turn off distractions. Do something that brings joy and rest. Thank God for His gift of stillness and delight.

You are seen, known, and loved—even in your silence.

Prayer

Lord of the Sabbath, thank You for the rhythm of rest. Teach me to delight in Your holy day and receive the joy it offers. Let stillness and joy meet in the sacred space of Sabbath. Amen.

78

The Gift of Boredom

Scripture Meditation

"Be still before the Lord and wait patiently for him." —
Psalm 37:7 (NIV)

We often run from boredom, filling empty space with noise and
distraction. But boredom can be a doorway to deeper presence if we
allow it.

Psalm 37 calls us to be still and wait patiently. Boredom stretches
us—it reveals what we rely on for stimulation and reminds us of our
hunger for purpose. Stillness, even when uncomfortable, invites us to
listen longer, look deeper, and be more present.

What feels boring might actually be sacred space in disguise. Embrace
it, and let the silence speak.

Reflection Questions

- How do you normally respond to moments of boredom or
  stillness
- What might God be inviting you to notice in those quiet spaces

Practice for Today

When you feel bored today, resist the urge to distract yourself. Sit in it for a few minutes. Ask God, 'What do You want to show me here?'

There is no rush. Heaven moves at the pace of peace.

"The quieter you become, the more you can hear." – Ram Dass

Prayer

God of silence and space, help me not to rush past boredom. Let it become a gift—an invitation to meet You in places I usually overlook. Teach me to wait and watch with patience. Amen.

79

Dying to Distraction

Scripture Meditation

"Set your minds on things above not on earthly things." — Colossians 3:2 (NIV)

Distraction is the enemy of depth. It scatters our attention and keeps us skimming the surface of life. But stillness teaches us to die to distraction so we can live fully present.

Paul exhorts us to set our minds on things above. This is not just a spiritual suggestion—it's a call to focus our lives on what truly matters. Stillness helps us name our distractions and let them go.

When we die to distraction, we are reborn to devotion. We learn to hear again, see again, feel again. We rediscover the sacred in what is simple and near.

Reflection Questions

- What distractions most often pull your heart and mind away from God
- How might stillness help you choose devotion over distraction

Practice for Today

Choose one distraction—your phone, a screen, a task—and fast from it for a few hours. Spend that time intentionally in quiet, prayer, or reflection with God.

God's presence is not far off; He is here in the quiet.

Prayer

Holy God, I confess how easily I'm pulled away from You. Teach me to die to distraction and live for Your presence. Let stillness reset my focus and renew my devotion. Amen.

OVERFLOW AND
TRANSFORMATION

80

When God Seems Silent

Scripture Meditation

> "The Lord is good to those whose hope is in him to the one who seeks him; it is good to wait quietly for the salvation of the Lord." — Lamentations 3:25–26 (NIV)

There are times when heaven feels quiet, and God seems distant. Prayers echo back empty, and we wonder if He's still listening. Yet even in the silence, God is present.

Lamentations teaches us that it is good to wait quietly. Silence is not always absence—it can be invitation. God often speaks in whispers, not shouts. And when He seems silent, He may be drawing us deeper into trust.

Stillness in these moments helps us stay rather than stray. It teaches us to seek Him not for answers, but for presence. And in that quiet, something holy grows.

Reflection Questions

- Have you experienced a season where God felt silent
- What sustained you or drew you deeper during that time

Practice for Today

If God feels silent today, don't rush away. Sit in stillness and simply repeat, 'I trust You.' Let the silence become sacred rather than scary.

Your soul is safe in the hands of the One who formed it.

Prayer

God of silence and presence, even when I do not hear You, I trust You are near. Help me to stay faithful in the quiet and find peace in Your unseen work. Amen.

81

Tuning the Heart to God

Scripture Meditation

"My heart says of you Seek his face! Your face Lord I will seek." — Psalm 27:8 (NIV)

Just as an instrument must be tuned to play true, our hearts must be tuned to hear God clearly. This doesn't happen in chaos—it happens in quiet.

David's prayer in Psalm 27 shows a heart that longs, listens, and seeks. Stillness makes space for this kind of tuning. It slows our thoughts and softens our hearts to respond to His voice.

To tune your heart is to come close. To turn down the noise of the world and align with the rhythm of heaven. Let stillness shape you into someone whose heart says every day, 'Your face, Lord, I will seek.'

Reflection Questions

- How do you know when your heart is in tune with God's
- What helps you return to that posture when you feel disconnected

Practice for Today

Spend a few minutes in stillness with your hand over your heart. As you breathe, whisper Psalm 27:8. Let your inner posture become one of seeking and soft surrender.

Your soul is safe in the hands of the One who formed it.

Prayer

God who draws near, tune my heart to hear You clearly. Let my soul respond to Your whispers. Align me with Your ways and make my seeking sincere. Amen.

82

Building a Life of Quiet Devotion

Scripture Meditation

"Make it your ambition to lead a quiet life you should mind your own business and work with your hands just as we told you." — 1 Thessalonians 4:11 (NIV)

In a world obsessed with platform and noise, Paul's words are refreshingly countercultural. A quiet life is not one of insignificance—it is one of focused devotion.

Stillness leads us to simplicity, and simplicity leads us to undistracted love. A quiet life makes room for God to be the centre, not the background.

Building a life of quiet devotion is a long obedience in the same direction. It is not flashy but faithful. And in its stillness, we become deeply rooted and richly nourished in Christ.

Reflection Questions

- What does a quiet and devoted life look like for you in this season
- What might God be inviting you to let go of to build that life more fully

Practice for Today

Reflect on your current lifestyle. Identify one area where you could choose simplicity and quiet devotion over noise or busyness. Take one step toward that shift today.

Your soul is safe in the hands of the One who formed it.

Prayer

Lord of quiet waters, help me build a life that honours You in stillness and devotion. Let my daily rhythms reflect Your peace and presence. Draw me into the joy of a quiet, holy life. Amen.

83

What Stillness Reveals

Scripture Meditation

"Search me God and know my heart test me and know my anxious thoughts. See if there is any offensive way in me and lead me in the way everlasting." — Psalm 139:23–24 (NIV)

Stillness is a mirror. When the noise fades and movement stops, what's inside begins to surface. In the quiet, God gently shows us what we've been too busy to see.

David's prayer in Psalm 139 is brave—he invites God to search and reveal. Stillness creates space for this courageous vulnerability. It's not always comfortable, but it is always healing.

What stillness reveals can lead us to repentance, restoration, and renewal. Let the quiet become a sacred space of transformation, where you are seen and shaped by love.

Reflection Questions

- What does stillness tend to reveal in your heart
- How do you respond when God brings something into the light

Practice for Today

Sit in stillness and pray Psalm 139:23–24. Write down anything the Holy Spirit brings to mind. Don't rush to fix—just notice and listen with openness.

"Be still and let Him mold you." – Brother Lawrence

Your soul is safe in the hands of the One who formed it.

Prayer

Loving God, thank You for seeing me fully and loving me completely. Search me in the stillness. Show me what needs healing, and lead me in Your everlasting way. Amen.

84

Rhythms of Withdrawal and Return

Scripture Meditation

"But Jesus often withdrew to lonely places and prayed." —
Luke 5:16 (NIV)

Jesus lived in rhythm—withdrawal and return. He retreated to
stillness and then returned to serve. This balance anchored His
ministry in intimacy, not activity.

Luke tells us that Jesus often withdrew. It wasn't an exception—it was
a rhythm. He knew that being poured out required being filled first.
Stillness was not a luxury for Him; it was essential.

We are called to the same pattern. To pull away in order to return with
grace. Let stillness become part of your sacred rhythm—where you
are renewed to re-enter the world with God's strength.

Reflection Questions

- Do you have regular rhythms of withdrawal and return in your
  life
- How could building this rhythm help you serve from overflow
  instead of exhaustion

Practice for Today

Schedule time this week to withdraw. Even one hour. Step away from your usual routine to pray or sit in stillness. Then return with fresh awareness of God's presence in your day.

There is no rush. Heaven moves at the pace of peace.

Prayer

Jesus, teach me the rhythm You lived. Help me withdraw often to find stillness and return with grace. May my life reflect Your pattern of communion and compassion. Amen.

85

Silence as a Spiritual Weapon

Scripture Meditation

"The Lord will fight for you; you need only to be still." —
Exodus 14:14 (NIV)

Silence doesn't feel like a weapon. In battle, we expect noise, strategy, and force. But in God's kingdom, stillness can be mightier than shouting.

In Exodus, as fear gripped the Israelites, Moses reminded them that stillness was their posture of power. God would fight. They were to be still.

Silence is not weakness—it is trust embodied. It is the refusal to be ruled by panic. In spiritual warfare, silence can shut the mouth of the enemy and open the ears of the heart.

Let stillness be your stance. Sometimes the most powerful thing you can do is stop striving, close your mouth, and believe that God will move.

Reflection Questions

• When do you feel most tempted to speak or act out of fear
• How could silence be a powerful response in those moments

Practice for Today

When faced with stress or confrontation today, pause. Breathe. Choose silence over reaction. Whisper Exodus 14:14 and trust God to speak and act on your behalf.

You are not behind—God meets you right where you are.

Prayer

Warrior God, help me to rely in Your strength. Let silence become a holy shield that declares You are fighting for me. Still my soul in every storm. Amen.

86

God's Silence in Scripture

Scripture Meditation

"Why Lord do you stand far off Why do you hide yourself in times of trouble" — Psalm 10:1 (NIV)

The Bible doesn't ignore silence. It wrestles with it. Again and again, the psalmists ask the hard question—Where are You, God?

God's silence is not rejection. It is often preparation. In Scripture, His pauses are purposeful. Joseph in the pit, Jesus in the tomb, Job in the ashes—each one experienced divine quiet before divine breakthrough.

Stillness helps us sit with the silence of God without fear. It teaches us to trust the Author even when the next chapter hasn't turned.

When God is silent, Scripture reminds us: He is still working. He is still good. He is still near.

Reflection Questions

• Have you ever felt confused by God's silence
• What biblical stories help you trust Him in the quiet

Practice for Today

Read a biblical story where God seemed silent—like Job, Joseph, or Jesus in Gethsemane. Reflect on how God was still present and active. Let that truth steady you today.

Your soul is safe in the hands of the One who formed it.

Prayer

God of mystery and mercy, help me to trust You even when I don't hear You. Let Scripture strengthen my faith in Your goodness and remind me that Your silence is never absence. Amen.

87

Learning to Love the Hiddenness

Scripture Meditation

"Truly you are a God who has been hiding himself the God and Savior of Israel." — Isaiah 45:15 (NIV)

There is a mystery to God's ways. He often works in hidden places, far from the spotlight. And while our souls long for clarity, faith grows best in the soil of trust.

Isaiah acknowledges that God sometimes hides Himself. Not to punish, but to deepen our pursuit. Hiddenness is an invitation—not to give up, but to go deeper.

Stillness draws us into that sacred obscurity. We stop demanding answers and start leaning into presence. We learn to love not just what God does, but who He is—even when unseen.

To love the hiddenness is to love the God who walks beside us in the dark, not just the light.

Reflection Questions

- How do you respond when God seems hidden or quiet
- What might He be forming in you during these hidden seasons

Practice for Today

Sit quietly with the truth that God is with you—even if hidden. Whisper Isaiah 45:15 as a prayer of faith, not frustration. Let His hiddenness deepen your hunger.

You don't have to earn God's nearness—just receive it.

Prayer

God who sometimes hides, help me to rely You in the dark. Help me to love You not only in clarity, but in mystery. Let stillness draw me deeper into Your hidden presence. Amen.

88

Practices for Everyday Stillness

Scripture Meditation

"Teach us to number our days that we may gain a heart of wisdom." — Psalm 90:12 (NIV)

Stillness doesn't only belong in the retreat or the prayer closet—it belongs in the ordinary. Wisdom is found when we pause and pay attention, even in the middle of a busy day.

Psalm 90 calls us to number our days—to live with awareness and intention. Stillness is the way we make time sacred. It's how we infuse divine presence into ordinary rhythms.

Whether it's a breath between tasks, a pause at a red light, or a moment of gratitude before meals, stillness can become woven into daily life. Let it be a habit of the heart, not just a spiritual luxury.

Reflection Questions

• Where can you create small pockets of stillness in your daily routine
• How could these moments help you grow in wisdom and awareness of God

Practice for Today

"In the cell of your soul, listen for the still, small voice." – St. Teresa of Avila

Choose one small action—like sipping your tea, folding laundry, or walking outside—and do it slowly and prayerfully today. Let it become a doorway to stillness and presence.

Your soul is safe in the hands of the One who formed it.

Prayer

Eternal God, help me to see You in the simple and the small. Teach me to live aware and present. Let stillness become a part of every hour, and wisdom grow in every breath. Amen.

89

Being vs Doing

Scripture Meditation

"Martha, Martha the Lord answered you are worried and upset about many things but few things are needed—or indeed only one. Mary has chosen what is better and it will not be taken away from her." — Luke 10:41–42 (NIV)

The world applauds doing—busyness, productivity, and constant movement. But Jesus points us to something deeper: being.

Martha was doing for Jesus. Mary was being with Him. One wasn't wrong, but one was better. Stillness invites us to sit at Jesus' feet, not because we have nothing to do, but because He is worthy of our full attention.

Doing flows best from being. We serve more purely when we're grounded in presence. Let stillness reset your soul—not by removing responsibility, but by reordering it.

Reflection Questions

- Do you tend to find your identity in doing or in being with God
- How can you practice choosing the 'better thing' like Mary today

Practice for Today

Before you begin your to-do list, take five minutes to simply be with Jesus. Sit in silence, breathe deeply, and acknowledge His presence. Let your day flow from that place of stillness.

You are not behind—God meets you right where you are.

Prayer

Jesus, teach me to choose what is better. Help me not to rush past Your presence in the name of productivity. Let my doing come from being with You. Amen.

90

Surrendering the Agenda

Scripture Meditation

"Many are the plans in a person's heart but it is the Lord's purpose that prevails." — Proverbs 19:21 (NIV)

We all carry agendas—lists, goals, expectations. They help us feel in control. But stillness invites us to lay them down.

Proverbs reminds us that our plans are many, but God's purpose is what lasts. Surrendering the agenda doesn't mean abandoning responsibility—it means inviting God to lead it all.

When we begin with stillness, we align our hearts with heaven. We ask not 'What do I want to accomplish?' but 'Lord, what are You doing today?' That shift changes everything.

Reflection Questions

- What plans or goals have you been holding tightly
- How might surrendering them bring you peace and alignment with God

Practice for Today

Before making decisions or starting your tasks today, pray, 'Not my will, but Yours be done.' Invite God to shape your plans and order your steps.

Your soul is safe in the hands of the One who formed it.

Prayer

Sovereign Lord, I surrender my plans and preferences. Lead me in Your purpose. Teach me to live with open hands and a still heart. Amen.

91

Hearing God Through Nature

Scripture Meditation

"The heavens declare the glory of God; the skies proclaim the work of his hands." — Psalm 19:1 (NIV)

God speaks through creation. The rustling leaves, the crashing waves, the quiet snowfall—all whisper His name. Stillness helps us tune in to nature's sermon.

Psalm 19 reminds us that the skies preach without words. When we pause and pay attention, we begin to hear God in birdsong and breeze. Nature becomes more than scenery—it becomes sanctuary.

Stillness outdoors can awaken worship. It reminds us we're small but seen, finite yet deeply loved. Let the world around you draw your heart to the One who made it.

Reflection Questions

- When was the last time you felt close to God in nature
- How can spending time in creation draw you into deeper stillness and awareness

Practice for Today

Take a short walk or sit outside in silence. Observe the details—light, colour, movement. Let creation become a window into the Creator's heart.

You are seen, known, and loved—even in your silence.

Prayer

Creator God, open my eyes to Your glory in the world around me. Let nature become my classroom and sanctuary. Draw me into stillness through the beauty of what You've made. Amen.

92

Monastic Rules for Quiet

Scripture Meditation

"Set a guard over my mouth Lord keep watch over the door of my lips." — Psalm 141:3 (NIV)

The early monastics understood that stillness wasn't just about silence of space—it was about silence of speech. They created rules to guide their tongues and protect the atmosphere of quiet devotion.

Psalm 141 reminds us that even our words need guarding. What we speak—or don't—can shape the soul's posture. Stillness often grows in the soil of intentional speech.

Monastic communities practiced periods of silence not to suppress, but to listen—to each other, to their hearts, and to God. We too can reclaim this sacred habit by choosing when to speak and when to simply be.

Reflection Questions

- How often do you pause before speaking
- How might intentional silence deepen your connection with God and others

Practice for Today

Commit to a one-hour silence window today. During that time, speak only when absolutely necessary. Let the quiet sharpen your awareness and deepen your peace.

You are invited into rest, not because you're finished, but because you are His.

Prayer

Lord, set a guard over my mouth and quiet my soul. Help me honour stillness with my speech. Let my silence become space for You to speak. Amen.

93

The Way of the Quiet Warrior

Scripture Meditation

"In repentance and rest is your salvation in quietness and trust is your strength." — Isaiah 30:15 (NIV)

The world celebrates loud leaders and fast victories. But God often raises warriors in quiet places. Their strength doesn't come from noise—but from trust.

Isaiah 30 points us to a paradox: strength through quietness. The quiet warrior is not passive—they are anchored. They fight, not with panic, but with peace. Their authority comes from intimacy with God, not applause from the crowd.

Stillness is not a retreat from the battle. It is preparation. It is the still heart that knows when to act and when to wait, when to speak and when to kneel.

Reflection Questions

• What does strength through quietness mean to you personally
• How can you cultivate stillness as part of your spiritual strength

Practice for Today

Spend five minutes visualising yourself as a quiet warrior—rooted, calm, focused. Ask God for strength through stillness and wisdom in every step you take.

"Withdraw into yourself and wait patiently." – The Desert Fathers

*Peace is not the absence of problems; it's the presence of God.

Prayer

Mighty God, train me in the way of the quiet warrior. Help me find strength in stillness, courage in trust, and power in peace. Make me bold without noise and faithful without fear. Amen.

94

Stillness in Leadership

Scripture Meditation

"Whoever wants to become great among you must be your servant and whoever wants to be first must be your slave."
— Matthew 20:26–27 (NIV)

Leadership often calls for action—but spiritual leadership calls first for presence. Jesus redefined greatness as servanthood, and stillness is where that posture is born.

The servant leader is not reactionary—they are rooted. They move with wisdom, not worry. Stillness trains leaders to listen before they speak, to discern before they direct.

Whether you lead a team, a family, or yourself, allow stillness shape your influence. Your quiet time with God is not a break from leadership—it is the beginning of it.

Reflection Questions

- How has stillness impacted your leadership
- Where might God be inviting you to lead more from rest than from reaction

Practice for Today

Before you make a leadership decision or respond to a challenge, pause. Sit in stillness for two minutes and ask, 'God, how do You want me to lead in this?'

Your soul is safe in the hands of the One who formed it.

Prayer

Jesus, servant King, teach me to lead from stillness. Let my authority be rooted in intimacy with You. Help me to lead like You—listening, loving, and laying down my life. Amen.

95

Clarity in the Quiet

Scripture Meditation

"Call to me and I will answer you and tell you great and unsearchable things you do not know." — Jeremiah 33:3 (NIV)

Noise confuses. Stillness clarifies. When the mind is crowded, discernment is dulled. But when we quiet the soul, we make room to hear the voice of wisdom.

Jeremiah 33 reminds us that God is eager to answer—He just waits for us to call. And often, His answers come not in the rush, but in the hush.

Stillness doesn't always give us immediate direction, but it prepares our hearts to receive it. In the quiet, confusion gives way to clarity, and fear gives way to trust.

Reflection Questions

- Where do you need clarity in your life right now
- How might stillness prepare you to hear God's answer more clearly

Practice for Today

Write out Jeremiah 33:3 and sit with it in stillness. Ask God for insight or direction in a specific area. Wait in silence, not for noise, but for peace.

Stillness is not weakness; it is strength in surrender.

Prayer

God who speaks in the quiet, I call to You. Still my heart so I can hear what You long to reveal. Let Your wisdom rise in the stillness and guide my steps. Amen.

96

A Garden Enclosed

Scripture Meditation

"You are a garden locked up my sister my bride; you are a spring enclosed a sealed fountain." — Song of Songs 4:12 (NIV)

There is a sacredness to hidden places. The imagery of a locked garden and sealed fountain in Song of Songs speaks to a life of intimacy, purity, and stillness before God.

Stillness is like a garden enclosed—it's not for public display, but private delight. It becomes a space where God walks with us, not for performance, but for love.

The world wants access to every part of us, but holiness begins with hiddenness. A life set apart, cultivated quietly, blooms with the fragrance of devotion.

Reflection Questions

- What parts of your spiritual life are cultivated in hiddenness
- How can you protect and nurture that sacred inner garden

Practice for Today

Take time today to retreat from noise and attention. Close the door. Sit in the quiet. Imagine your soul as a garden where God desires to dwell.

Peace is not the absence of problems; it's the presence of God.

Prayer

Lover of my soul, let my heart be a garden enclosed—yours alone. Help me protect what is sacred. Walk with me in the quiet, and may my life bloom in Your presence. Amen.

97

The Beauty of the Unspoken

Scripture Meditation

"Even before a word is on my tongue behold O Lord you know it altogether." — Psalm 139:4 (ESV)

Some of the most sacred things are never said aloud. God sees them anyway. He knows the word before it is spoken, the prayer before it's formed.

Stillness honours the unspoken. It trusts that we don't need to fill every silence with speech. In the hush, there is reverence—a recognition that God is here, even when words fall short.

There is beauty in what remains unsaid, holiness in the quiet ache or silent joy. Let your stillness today become a sanctuary where the unspoken is received and understood by God.

Reflection Questions

- What prayer or thought have you kept silent, yet long for God to hear
- How does it feel to know He understands the unspoken parts of your heart

Practice for Today

Sit in silence for five minutes. Don't speak, don't write—just be. Let your silence become a prayer, knowing that God hears everything you cannot say.

You are invited into rest, not because you're finished, but because you are His.

Prayer

Lord, You know me better than I know myself. Hear my silence and receive it as worship. Meet me in the spaces beyond language and speak to the depths of my soul. Amen.

98

Returning to the Center

Scripture Meditation

"Come to me all you who are weary and burdened and I will give you rest. Take my yoke upon you and learn from me for I am gentle and humble in heart and you will find rest for your souls." — Matthew 11:28–29 (NIV)

Life pulls us in many directions. Responsibilities, distractions, ambitions—they scatter our souls. Stillness is how we return to the centre where Jesus waits.

His invitation is not complex. It's not for the perfect or the put-together. It's for the weary and burdened. It's an open door to rest and renewal.

Returning to the centre isn't about running away from life—it's about grounding it in Him. Let stillness lead you back today. Not to a place, but to a Person.

Reflection Questions

- Where do you feel scattered or worn thin right now
- What would it look like to return to Jesus as your center today?

Practice for Today

Close your eyes and breathe deeply. Imagine laying your burdens at Jesus' feet. Whisper, 'You are my centre.' Let everything else fade for just a few moments.

"Let nothing disturb you, let nothing frighten you, all things are passing." – St. Teresa of Avila

Your soul is safe in the hands of the One who formed it.

Prayer

Jesus, I return to You weary and burdened. Be my centre again. Quiet the noise and gather the scattered pieces of my soul. Let me find rest in You alone. Amen.

99

Holy Detachment

Scripture Meditation

"But whatever were gains to me I now consider loss for the sake of Christ." — Philippians 3:7 (NIV)

To detach is not to stop caring—it is to stop clinging. Holy detachment is the practice of loosening our grip on everything that is not God.

Paul's words in Philippians reflect this surrender. What once seemed like gain now fades in light of Christ. Stillness allows this shift to happen in us—not through striving, but release.

Holy detachment makes room for holy affection. As we let go, we are free to receive more of God. And in that freedom, we discover the deepest kind of stillness: contentment in Him alone.

Reflection Questions

- What are you holding onto too tightly in this season
- How might releasing it open you up to greater intimacy with God

Practice for Today

Hold your hands out, palms up. Imagine what you need to release into God's hands. Speak it aloud, then say, 'Christ is enough for me.'

God's presence is not far off; He is here in the quiet.

Prayer

Jesus, I let go of what I've been gripping too tightly. I count all things loss compared to knowing You. Fill the empty spaces with Your peace. You are more than enough. Amen.

100

Becoming Still _ Living a Life Anchored in God

Scripture Meditation

> "He says Be still and know that I am God; I will be exalted among the nations I will be exalted in the earth." — Psalm 46:10 (NIV)

Stillness is not merely a moment—it's a becoming. It's the fruit of a life anchored in Christ's presence, surrendered to His rhythm, and anchored in His love.

Psalm 46:10 echoes through this entire journey: 'Be still and know.' This knowing is not intellectual—it is intimate. It is the quiet confidence that comes from dwelling with God.

To become still is to carry peace into every place. It is to live from the centre, not the edges. And it is to know—deep in your bones—that no matter what storms may come, you are held.

Let your life become a sanctuary of stillness, a testimony to the God who is near, and a wellspring of peace to the world around you.

Reflection Questions

- How has your understanding of stillness deepened through this journey
- What practices will you carry forward to remain anchored in God

Practice for Today

Find a quiet place. Read Psalm 46 slowly. Reflect on what it means to live anchored in God. Write a prayer or declaration about the still life you long to live.

Prayer

Father, I'm grateful for the blessing of stillness. Anchor me in Your love. Let my life reflect the quiet strength of Your presence. May I live from rest, led by peace, and known by You. Amen.

A Personal Commission

You have walked through stillness—chapter by chapter, breath by breath. You have made space for God in your silence and let Him draw near in the quiet. This is not the end. It is the beginning of a new way of being.

You are now commissioned to carry stillness into your daily life. Let it be your rhythm, your strength, your sanctuary. Let your presence be a refuge for others. Let your stillness preach louder than words. Wherever you go, carry peace.

Reader's Benediction

May the quiet places call you often.

May your heart find rest beneath the noise.

May you hear God's whisper in the silence,

And know that He is near.

May stillness become your sanctuary,

Peace your companion,

And presence your strength.

You are deeply loved,

Forever held,

And always welcome in the quiet heart of God.

Amen.

Bibliography

The Holy Bible, New International Version (NIV). Biblica, Inc.

The Holy Bible, New King James Version (NKJV). Thomas Nelson, Inc.

The Holy Bible, English Standard Version (ESV). Crossway.

Teresa of Avila. *The Interior Castle*. Translated by Mirabai Starr, Riverhead Books, 2003.

St. Augustine. *Confessions*. Translated by R.S. Pine-Coffin, Penguin Classics, 1961.

Thomas Merton. *New Seeds of Contemplation*. New Directions, 2007.`'~

John of the Cross. *Dark Night of the Soul*. Translated by Mirabai Starr, Riverhead Books, 2002.

Henri Nouwen. The Way of the Heart: Connecting with God through Prayer, Wisdom, and Silence. HarperOne, 2003.

Richard Foster. *Celebration of Discipline: The Path to Spiritual Growth*. HarperOne, 1998.

Dallas Willard. *The Spirit of the Disciplines: Understanding How God Changes Lives*. HarperOne, 1988.

Brother Lawrence. *The Practice of the Presence of God*. Whitaker House, 1982.

Ruth Haley Barton. *Invitation to Solitude and Silence: Experiencing God's Transforming Presence*. InterVarsity Press, 2004.

John Mark Comer. *The Ruthless Elimination of Hurry*. WaterBrook, 2019.

Peter Scazzero. *Emotionally Healthy Spirituality*. Zondervan, 2006.

The Sayings of the Desert Fathers. Translated by Benedicta Ward, Cistercian Publications, 1984.